"A first-rate piece of work. This treatment of the eucharistic prayer is both respectable and very accessible. It should be very helpful in catechizing for the new translation of the Mass."

—John F. Baldovin, SJ
Professor of Historical & Liturgical Theology
Boston College School of Theology and Ministry

"Barry Hudock rightly points out that 'the most fundamental thing the church has to say to God is "thank you."' The church's great prayer of thanksgiving is often perceived, however, as a low point at Mass, often because priest and people have not reflected on the meaning, history, and content of the eucharistic prayers. With his perspective of this prayer as a doxological proclamation of the gospel, Hudock provides a well-documented, yet quite readable study of the history and component parts of the Roman Rite's multiple eucharistic prayers and offers reflections on the special thrust of each of the prayers currently in use. To conclude, Hudock links liturgy with life and offers his thoughts on developing an authentic contemporary spirituality based on the eucharistic prayer."

—Dennis C. Smolarski, SJ
Author of *Eucharist and American Culture*
and *How Not to Say Mass: A Guidebook on
Liturgical Principals and the Roman Missal*

The Eucharistic Prayer

A User's Guide

Barry Hudock

Foreword by Rev. Msgr. Kevin W. Irwin

LITURGICAL PRESS
Collegeville, Minnesota

www.litpress.org

1   2   3   4   5   6   7   8   9

Library of Congress Cataloging-in-Publication Data

Hudock, Barry.
   The eucharistic prayer : a user's guide / Barry Hudock.
     p. cm.
   ISBN 978-0-8146-3287-1 — ISBN 978-0-8146-3935-1 (e-book)
  1. Eucharistic prayers—Catholic Church.   I. Title.
   BX2015.6.H83   2010
   264'.02036—dc22
                                       2010017257

In no way could this be dedicated to just one person.
So this is for a handful of people for whom I give thanks daily:
my mother, Judy, now gone to God;
my father, Mike, and his wife Margaret;
my wife, Toni, my treasure and fellow-traveler;
and our children:
Abigail, Cecilia, Nicholas, Hope, Gianna, Jacob, and Brittany.

Contents

Foreword

This is a modest book by a modest man. Insightful without being ponderous, challenging without being off-putting, engaging without being showy, authoritative without being officious—all phrases that can be written about this book and about its author!

It is a remarkable work in that it goes far beyond its origin—a requirement for an advanced degree in the Liturgical Studies Program at The Catholic University of America. In the intervening years since it was first penned, Barry Hudock has continued to research and reflect on what is indeed the center and summit of the entire act of Eucharist. This additional work and insight is on every page. As is his passion. That industry and enthusiasm are infectious and resonate well with the educated (not necessarily theologically conversant) audience intended.

Throughout, the reader is invited to learn, to reflect, and then to return to the celebration of the Eucharist with deeper insight and care. Anyone who reads this book with attention and openness will profit beyond words—literally—even the words of the eucharistic prayer. What will likely result are changed hearts and more devoted lives lived in the Lord whose memorial is at the heart of this prayer.

At a time in the church's life when restrained rhetoric is often jettisoned in favor of hyperbole, not to say rancorous speech, Hudock accomplishes his task placidly yet tenaciously. He wants to communicate what he believes. And what he believes is derived from what the church itself says and prays about the Eucharist. What better source for theology, spirituality, and action than the church's own *lex orandi*. For example he skillfully reflects on the institution narrative (in chap. 7) to invite us to consider real presence, sacrifice, covenant, and love all at the same time and all in relation to each other as well as to the narrative of the Last Supper.

In an age when "spirituality" is hot copy but not always theologically influenced or in any way profound, Hudock's treatment of a eucharistic spirituality in chapter 18 is a model of what can be gleaned from the church's prayer when led by a skilled guide such as Hudock and a person who is obviously attuned to what the Eucharist does, is, and means in daily life.

As Hudock argues well, the Eucharist is about a number of things, but "blessing" and "thanksgiving" are at the top. Thanks to the man who has produced what is nothing short of a blessing for the church in writing this book. Indeed a modest book by a modest man.

Rev. Msgr. Kevin W. Irwin
Dean
School of Theology and Religious Studies
The Catholic University of America
Washington DC

Acknowledgments

The following people had a hand, in one way or another, in the preparation of this book. I offer them all my enthusiastic thanks.

- ❑ Father John O'Connor, a faithful and supportive friend;
- ❑ The extraordinary community of Christian Brothers Academy in Syracuse, New York, especially Brother Thomas Zoppo, SFC, Joe Assaf, and Marilyn Goulet;
- ❑ Bishop Donald Trautman, a good shepherd;
- ❑ The professors of the School of Religious Studies at the Catholic University of America, in particular Monsignor Kevin Irwin (who directed the thesis that was the seed from which this book grew), Father Gerard Austin, OP, and Sister Mary Collins, OSB, each of whom broadened my vision;
- ❑ Jeffery BeBeau, for generously sharing a back issue of *Notitiae* with a stranger.

Thanks most of all to Toni and our children for their generous patience, support, and cooperation, because every moment I spent on this book was a moment less spent with them.

Introduction:
"We Should Wear Crash Helmets"

The seed that grew into this book was a thesis I wrote while pursuing an STL in sacramental theology at the Catholic University of America. I was a priest of the diocese of Erie, Pennsylvania, at the time, sent by my bishop for graduate studies. My topic was the history and theology of Eucharistic Prayer II of the 1969 Roman Missal (the Mass as it was reformed after Vatican II). I was amazed and excited by all that I learned during the research and writing about that prayer, but also about the nature and history of the eucharistic prayer in general.

Fast forward more than a decade. I'm laicized and married now, with one stepchild and six more children of my own. I presently work as the director of two nonprofit agencies that help people living in poverty in southern West Virginia (one by providing direct aid in emergency situations, the other by confronting systemic causes of poverty). Given these significant changes, it might have been understandable for my particular interest in the eucharistic prayer (which is not to say the Eucharist) to have been left by the wayside along life's journey.

But it never has, not for a moment. In fact, life as a layman, following life as a priest, has provided a unique perspective on the eucharistic prayer. After all, it's one thing to pray the prayer as a priest, entirely another to pray it as a layperson.

It's not difficult to engage your mind and heart while standing in the center of the sanctuary before a congregation, personally enunciating all the words, extending your hands and arms, holding the host in your own fingers, lifting a chalice that's your own, never more clearly acting as priest.

To kneel in the pew among a church full of other pew-kneelers, quiet and still, with your own restless children (one upset that a sibling got to put the money in the basket, another just ready to go home) at your sides—that is a different matter. I'm rarely as attentive and engaged as I would like to be, and it's more work to even get close. But I at least bring a theological background that makes me keenly aware of the importance of what is going on, that I can draw upon as I listen to the priest move through his recitation of the prayer, and that teaches me the extraordinary part that I—along with all those around me in the pews—am called to play.

But most folks don't. Most Catholics, if asked about the eucharistic prayer, would probably be able to say something about the words of consecration being important. I suspect many would add something about it being "the prayer the priest prays."

Pulitzer Prize-winner Annie Dillard had it right, reflecting on her own experience of parish worship, that most of us "do not seem to have the foggiest idea what sort of power we so blithely invoke" when we gather. "The churches," she wrote, "are children playing on the floor with their chemistry sets, making up a batch of TNT to kill a Sunday morning. It is madness to wear ladies' hats and straw hats and velvet hats to church; we should all be wearing crash helmets. Ushers should issue life preservers and signal flares; they should lash us to our pews."[1]

When it comes to the eucharistic prayer, she's right on the money. And yet, the *General Instruction for the Roman Missal* (GIRM; that's the church's instruction book on the Mass) calls the eucharistic prayer "the high point of the entire celebration."[2] So I thought it might be a good idea to put together some thoughts that might help the average, educated, pew-sitting (and pew-

1. Annie Dillard, *Teaching a Stone to Talk: Expeditions and Encounters* (New York: Harper Colophon, 1982), 40.

2. GIRM 30.

kneeling, since we're talking about the eucharistic prayer here) Catholic understand its riches more deeply.

Please note: I love the study of theology, but I'm no professional scholar. I'm not writing here for scholars, and this book does not represent my own original research and thinking. I acknowledge a weighty debt to many scholars, whose work I have tried to present here in an accessible, compelling, and clear form.

In particular, the fascinating work of Enrico Mazza permeates this book. Mazza is surely the most authoritative living expert on the history, development, and theology of the eucharistic prayer. Particularly important to my research were his three books, *The Eucharistic Prayers of the Roman Rite* (Pueblo, 1986), *The Origins of the Eucharistic Prayer* (Liturgical Press, 1995), and *The Celebration of the Eucharist: The Origin of the Rite and the Development of Its Interpretation* (Liturgical Press, 1999). Other scholars, too, some living and some dead, have helped me along the way. In particular, Joseph Jungmann, Cipriano Vagaggini, Louis Bouyer, Alexander Schmemann, Max Thurian, Joseph Ratzinger, and Paul Bradshaw have been helpful. Their influence will be recognizable in these pages to those who know their work. Of course, whatever I flub here I managed to do all on my own.

But my premise here is that an understanding of the eucharistic prayer needn't be the exclusive privilege of scholars and certainly should not be limited to the clergy. The Second Vatican Council's Constitution on the Sacred Liturgy (*Sacrosanctum Concilium*) called for all Catholics to "take part [in the liturgy] fully aware of what they are doing, actively engaged in the rite, and enriched by its effects."[3] One would think that would apply in a particular way to "the center and summit of the entire celebration" of Mass,[4] which is also how GIRM speaks of the eucharistic prayer.

❏ ❏ ❏

3. SC 11. Translation from Austin Flannery, OP, *Vatican Council II: The Conciliar and Post Conciliar Documents*, 1988 rev. ed. (Boston: St. Paul Editions, 1987).

4. GIRM 78.

Here's my plan.

In Part One we'll get an overview of what the eucharistic prayer is all about. Chapter 1 will consider the dual question, "What is the eucharistic prayer, and why should I care?" Chapter 2 will ask, "Who prays the eucharistic prayer?" (The answer may be a bit more interesting, and more beautiful, than you think.) Then in Chapter 3 we'll take a brief look at the interesting history of the eucharistic prayer.

If Part One was sort of like taking a walk around the car, inspecting the body and kicking the tires a bit, Part Two is about lifting up the hood and taking a look underneath. We'll go through the prayer part by part (see GIRM 79), exploring how it's put together and considering what each piece is about, what it "does."

In Part Three we'll take a good look at the four primary eucharistic prayers in use in the Roman rite today. Most practicing Catholics are probably aware that there are four but may not know much more about them beyond the fact that one is short (the one we hear most often), one is long (we never hear that one), and another one is also pretty long, largely because of those big lists of saints' names! That's unfortunate, because, as Pope Benedict XVI has written, they are "noteworthy for their inexhaustible theological and spiritual richness."[5] We'll also look at the other eucharistic prayers found in the Roman Missal.

And finally, in Part Four we'll look more closely at the important connections that are suggested by these prayers between the liturgy we celebrate in church and the lives we live outside of Mass.

◻ ◻ ◻

At the end of my work on that degree in sacramental theology I mentioned above, I sat for my oral comprehensive exam. One of the examiners, Fr. Michael Witzak, posed a question to me

---

5. Pope Benedict XVI, *Sacramentum Caritatis*: *Post-Synodal Apostolic Exhortation on the Eucharist as the Source and Summit of the Church's Life and Mission* (February 22, 2007), 48.

about those comments from the GIRM, that the eucharistic prayer is "the high point" and "the center and summit of the entire celebration" of Mass. He asked, "If we asked several Catholics coming out of church on Sunday morning what the high point of the Mass they'd just attended was, what do you think they would say?"

I had to admit that some would mention the consecration (which is, to be sure, a part of the eucharistic prayer) or receiving Communion (which is not); others, depending on the skills of the preacher, would probably point to the homily; a few others, if they were honest, might smile sheepishly and admit that it was, for them, the dismissal. I was interested to find more recently, in fact, that in a multiparish series of interviews with Mass-going Catholics in the early 1990s the majority of people interviewed cited the Sign of Peace or holding hands during the recitation of the Lord's Prayer as the high point of the liturgy they had just attended.[6]

How many would answer that it was the eucharistic prayer? Would you? I wouldn't have, not before I had the opportunity to take a much closer look at it, at what Catholic liturgical tradition reveals about it, at what the church teaches about it, and at what the research of many skilled theologians and historians has discerned about its history and meaning.

"Well, what can we do about that?" Fr. Witzak asked. I suppose this book is part of a response to the challenge implicit in that question.

On the other hand, it might be best to leave things the way they are. They start handing out crash helmets and signal flares at Mass, and I'll never be able to control my kids.

---

6. Cf. John Baldovin, "Pastoral Liturgical Reflections on the Study," *The Awakening Church: Twenty-five Years of Liturgical Renewal*, ed. Lawrence J. Madden (Collegeville, MN: Liturgical Press, 1992), 104.

The Eucharistic Prayer

What Is the Eucharistic Prayer, and What Is So August, Stark, Sacred, Majestic, and Awesome about It Anyway?

"We are entering into the august, stark, sacred, majestic, awesome sanctuary of the eucharistic prayers."[1]

These are not the words of a medieval pope, back in the days when the priest and what he does at the altar, out of earshot and nearly out of sight of the people in the pews, were somehow on a completely different level of existence from the bric-a-brac of life. This is Pope Paul VI, addressing a meeting of Italian liturgists on February 7, 1969. The Second Vatican Council was over and the work of reforming the Roman Catholic liturgy it had called for was well underway. Three new eucharistic prayers had just been introduced into the Roman rite, and they could be prayed, for the first time in many centuries, both loud enough to be heard by the people assembled for Mass and in their own language. Reforms had been introduced that would make the Eucharist much more clearly an action of the assembly, and the trend was to emphasize these elements of the liturgy.

But Paul VI—not a man who was inclined to melodrama or exaggeration in his public statements—insisted that February day on using a sequence of five vibrant adjectives when it came to the eucharistic prayer.

What is the eucharistic prayer, and why did he feel it merited such words?

---

1. *Documents on the Liturgy 1963–1979: Conciliar, Papal and Curial Texts* (Collegeville, MN: Liturgical Press, 1982), 621 (DOL 246).

Where It Is

The eucharistic prayer is one part of the Mass, the structure of which (in today's Roman rite) looks like this:

❑ Introductory Rites (greeting, penitential act, Gloria, collect)
❑ Liturgy of the Word (first reading, responsorial psalm, second reading, alleluia, gospel reading, homily, creed, prayers of the faithful)
❑ Liturgy of the Eucharist (preparation of the gifts, eucharistic prayer, Lord's Prayer, distribution of Communion, prayer after Communion)
❑ Concluding Rites (final blessing, dismissal)

The eucharistic prayer is the central part of the Liturgy of the Eucharist. It opens with a dialogue between priest and people:

℣: The Lord be with you.
℟: And with your spirit.
℣: Lift up your hearts.
℟: We lift them up to the Lord.
℣: Let us give thanks to the Lord our God.
℟: It is right and just.

It ends with people and presider together proclaiming the great Amen. Everything in between is included in the eucharistic prayer.

What It Is

But what *is* it?

The eucharistic prayer is *the church's prayer of thanksgiving and offering, prayed over the gifts offered in the celebration of the Eucharist.* It is also known, particularly in the East, as the *anaphora* (from the Greek for "lifting up" or "offering"), and the two terms will be used interchangeably in this book.

The eucharistic prayer is *the central and definitive liturgical expression of the church's faith.* If the Bible is the Gospel in narrative form, and the *Catechism of the Catholic Church* is the Gospel in doctrinal form, so the eucharistic prayer is *the Gospel proclaimed doxologically, that is, in the form of liturgical praise, thanksgiving, and offering.*[2]

Here the church proclaims not only what happened to Jesus at the end of his earthly life but also what those events mean to humanity *and* how those events and their meaning are "actualized here and now in an ever new experience of grace through the paschal mystery."[3] It is Jesus' Paschal Mystery, his death and resurrection, transformed by him into verbal form, into a public, corporate prayer.[4]

The Law of Prayer

How can we justify claiming for this prayer such an important role? A good place to start is with an ancient Christian axiom: *lex orandi, lex credendi.* "The law of prayer is the law of belief." The liturgy, in other words, is an authoritative expression of the church's faith. The words we pray and the things we do there carry theological and doctrinal weight.[5]

Though classical, this is actually the bumper-sticker version of a principle first expressed by a fifth-century monk named Prosper of Aquitaine. Prosper was intensely involved in confronting the Pelagian and semi-Pelagian beliefs of his day, which suggested that our salvation is not a gift of grace, but rather the earned result of our own efforts and determination. Defending the church's teaching that the grace of God is necessary for salvation, Prosper cited the prayers for various people and groups in the Good Friday liturgy and the prebaptismal exorcisms as proof of the church's

2. Cf. Aidan Kavanagh, "Thoughts on the New Eucharistic Prayers," in R. Kevin Seasoltz, ed., *Living Bread, Saving Cup: Readings on the Eucharist* (Collegeville, MN: Liturgical Press, 1987), 105–6.

3. Kevin Irwin, *Context and Text: Method in Liturgical Theology* (Collegeville, MN: Liturgical Press, 1994), 180.

4. Cf. Joseph Cardinal Ratzinger, *God Is Near Us: The Eucharist, The Heart of Life,* tr. Henry Taylor (San Francisco: Ignatius Press, 2003), 49.

5. *Context and Text,* 3–6. Cf. Alexander Schmemann, *Introduction to Liturgical Theology,* tr. Asheleigh E. Moorehouse (Crestwood, NY: St. Vladimir's Seminary Press, 1996), 10–27; Thomas Fisch, ed., *Liturgy and Tradition: Theological Reflections of Alexander Schmemann* (Crestwood, NJ: St. Vladimir's Seminary Press, 1990), 16–68.

faith in their need for God's grace. Explaining his approach, he asserted: *legem credendi lex statuat supplicandi.* "The law of prayer establishes the law of belief."

Prosper didn't invent the principle, though. He was simply the first to articulate it so clearly. From early Christian history the liturgy has been recognized as a means by which the orthodox faith is manifested and transmitted in a reliable and authoritative way. For example:

- Against the Arian heretics who maintained that Christ was not truly divine, St. Athanasius and other fourth-century defenders of the church's teaching pointed out the inconsistency of the Arians' worship of Christ in the liturgy and their refusal to acknowledge his full divinity in their doctrine.
- In the fifth century, Alexandrian theologians such as Cyril defended their doctrine on the Eucharist (that the bread and wine become "the very flesh of the Logos") against Antiochene explanations (which maintained that by faith the bread and wine subjectively become the body of Christ to the believer) by arguing that their own teaching conformed to the faith expressed and practiced in the church's liturgy, while the Antiochenes' did not.
- When Christians around the same time debated the appropriateness of the title "*theotokos*" (God-bearer or Mother of God) for Mary, the fact that it was already firmly established in Christian worship argued strongly in its favor.

In each case defenders of the faith of the church made essentially the same argument that had been offered by St. Irenaeus of Lyons, in his second-century disputation against Gnostic dualists (who rejected both the resurrection of the body and the goodness of creation): "[O]ur opinion agrees with the eucharist and the eucharist, in turn, establishes our opinion."[6]

---

6. *Against Heresies* 4:18:5, in Daniel J. Sheerin, *The Eucharist* (Wilmington, DE: Michael Glazier, 1986), 249. The passage is quoted in the *Catechism of the Catholic Church* 1327.

Though this understanding was neglected for many centuries, it was never completely forgotten. (Thirteenth-century theological giant St. Thomas Aquinas regarded liturgy as a significant authority in the formation of Catholic theology, and Pope Sixtus V referred to the *lex orandi* principle in his teaching in 1587.)[7] In the twentieth century the idea received renewed appreciation by both theologians and the magisterium.[8]

The Work of Our Redemption

But the liturgy does more than teach us about the faith. By its very nature faith cannot be contained in a book. Faith is not an idea, or at any rate not *only* an idea. To believe that God exists, or that a certain set of statements about him is true, is not faith. "Even the demons believe . . . and tremble" (Jas 2:19)! God does not reveal himself to humanity by publishing a list of his personal attributes.

The faith of the church is not founded simply on facts, but on certain historical events. Through these events—for Israel it was primarily the Passover-Exodus event; for the church it was the life and especially the death and resurrection of Jesus—God was encountered in a definitive way. The God of the Bible, of both testaments, is not simply God-who-is-understood, but God-with-us, God-encountered, God-who-saves.[9] Faith, then, necessarily involves experience, an act that is never solely a personal human act but also a divine act. Faith is the encounter-in-event of a person (or a community) with the living God, a giving of oneself to God encountered, and the communion of oneself with God that flows from such an encounter. It can never be adequately expressed in a given statement or set of statements accepted as true.

With this in mind, the important relationship between Christian faith and Christian liturgy becomes clearer. Liturgy is not an

7. *Context and Text*, 25, 27.

8. Cf. ibid., 18–32.

9. Cf. Joseph Cardinal Ratzinger, *Principles of Catholic Theology: Building Stones for a Fundamental Theology*, tr. Mary Frances McCarthy (San Francisco: Ignatius Press, 1987), 153–90.

object or fact. Liturgy happens. It is "a theological event. In essence, liturgy is an act of theology, an act whereby the believing church addresses God, enters into dialogue with God, makes statements about its belief in God and symbolizes this belief through a variety of means including creation, words, manufactured objects, ritual gestures and actions."[10] It is the "church's faith in motion."[11] Liturgy is an event in the life of the people of God, the function of which is to call to mind and make present the very elements on which their faith is founded.

And so the liturgy speaks of itself, and of the Eucharist in particular, as being an act in which "the work of our redemption is accomplished."[12] The mysteries about which we speak, the redemption for which we give thanks, are made real and effective in the liturgy. "No other action of the Church can equal its [the liturgy's] efficacy by the same title and to the same degree" (SC 7).

At the Center of the Center

If all of this applies to the church's liturgy in general, it applies in a particular way to its eucharistic prayer. I've already quoted, in the Introduction, *GIRM*'s teaching that the eucharistic prayer is "the high point" and the "center and summit of the entire celebration"[13] of the Mass. Put that conviction alongside *Sacrosanctum Concilium*'s insistence that the Eucharist is the source and summit of the church's life, and that puts the eucharistic prayer in an interesting place: *at the center of the center* of everything, the heart of the heart of life.

This is expressed in the early Christians' awareness of the eucharistic prayer as the essential ritual act, so much so that the name of this particular prayer only later became the name for

10. *Context and Text*, 44.

11. Aidan Kavanagh, *On Liturgical Theology* (New York: Pueblo, 1984), 8

12. From the prayer over the gifts, Holy Thursday evening liturgy. The phrase is cited in *Sacrosanctum Concilium* 2 (though at the time of the document's promulgation, before the liturgical reform it called for, the phrase was from the Secret prayer of the ninth Sunday after Pentecost). Cf. *Context and Text*, 186 n. 45.

13. *GIRM* 30, 78.

the entire celebration: *eucharist*. It is expressed in the practice of medieval theologians reflecting and commenting on the words of the Roman Canon as they did passages of Scripture.

In the eucharistic prayer, with an intensity and an effectiveness like that in no other moment of Christian worship, we give thanks for God's wonderworks, creation and redemption; we join the angels of heaven in their eternal and perfect praise of the glory of God; we call down the Holy Spirit and ask him to transform both the gifts we offer and us; by the Spirit's power we make Christ present that we may receive his very being; we join with Christ in the eternal offering of himself to his eternal Father; we intercede as the church for the church.

So there's a lot to get excited about, for Paul VI as well as for us. And we've only scratched the surface so far. Let's continue our investigation of the eucharistic prayer, "this iridescent robe, this sacred vestment in which the whole universe is reflected around the Church and her heavenly Bridegroom."[14]

---

14. Louis Bouyer, *Eucharist: Theology and Spirituality of the Eucharistic Prayer*, tr. Charles Underhill Quinn (Notre Dame, IN: University of Notre Dame Press, 1968), 2.

Who Prays the Eucharistic Prayer?
An Extraordinary Answer

The priest does. Duh.

Next chapter.

Ah, but wait a moment. Okay, it's true: the words of the eucharistic prayer—most of them, anyway—come from the mouth of the guy standing up front in the colorful robes. But now that we have acknowledged the obvious, let's take another look. You'll be glad we did, because looking at the liturgy with the eyes of faith—through the triple lenses of Christian liturgical tradition, Sacred Scripture, and Catholic doctrine—reveals far more to see and talk about here. And the view is rather astounding.

Two extremes, almost caricatures of positions, float around out there in the Catholic world, posing as answers to the question this chapter asks. Like most extremes, they're to be avoided, because both ignore some data that's crucial to forming a well-grounded answer.

One position goes something like this: We all do. We need a priest to preside at our liturgies just as we need a moderator for an online chat. But in this chat room everyone has a voice and no one dominates the conversation. The priest's role is not unique, for we are all "other Christs" by baptism, and in these difficult days of "priestless Sundays" we need to get used to the fact that we're just going to have to do without 'em. Sister Sarah is a better preacher than Father Finegan ever was anyway.

The other position sounds like this: The priest does. The Catholic faithful are bound by divine law to attend Mass every Sunday (and receive Communion once a year). But what they do in their pews is not nearly as important as what's being done in the sanctuary before them. A divine drama plays out there, and the priest is the protagonist. The people in the pews are an audience, fortunate to be present for such an awesome act of God, passive receivers of what is being done *for* them and given *to* them through the ministry of God's priest.

An authentic Catholic approach to the question is more nuanced than either of those.

Christ the Priest

A good place to start thinking through all this is here: *neither* the presiding priest *nor* the gathered people are the primary offerers or celebrants of the Mass. That role belongs to Christ himself. Within the very life of the Holy Trinity, Christ offers himself eternally, in the unity of the Spirit, to the Father. Liturgy—in fact, all Christian prayer—is fundamentally *our participation in that*.

To be sure, properly understood, there is a rich and worthy place in Christian tradition for prayer and worship directed to Christ. The same can be said for prayer to the Holy Spirit. At the same time, we have to be wary of a sort of practical tritheism in it, the suggestion that God the Father, God the Son, and God the Holy Spirit are three gods, with whom a person might have three distinct and separate relationships. An awareness that all our prayer is through Christ, in the unity of the Spirit, to the Father safeguards our faith in God's oneness.

But don't take my word for it. Consider St. Paul. There are few passages of Scripture that are so beautifully christocentric as the famous hymn in Philippians 2:6-11. Here Christ's divinity and his lordship over the entire universe are enthusiastically proclaimed. When Paul says that "at the name of Jesus every knee should bend, in heaven and on earth and under the earth" (2:10), an Old Testament aficionado (like Paul, who started out a very devout Jew) hears a clear echo of Isaiah 45:23, in which God claims that all worship on earth belongs to God.[1] And the acclamation of what may be the earliest Christian creed, "Jesus Christ is Lord," particularly in the context of the entire hymn, is an unambiguous acknowledgment of Christ's divinity.

And yet, among those climactic lines, almost lost in the exuberance, is another important phrase—Paul's insistence that this exaltation of Christ, and even the proclamation of him as Lord, is done "to the glory of God the Father."

Or consider the most liturgical of the New Testament books, the letter to the Hebrews, whose primary theme is the priesthood of Christ.[2] The letter makes clear that Christ's priesthood was not assumed by him but *received* by him from God (the Father) (5:1-10). And it is *through* Christ the priest that people draw near to God: "He at all times is able to save those who come to God through him, since he lives always to make intercession for them" (Heb 7:25; see also 10:19-22 and 13:15).

In the vision of the author of the letter to the Hebrews, Christ is the "one liturgist" of the "one liturgy" offered to the Father in the "one sanctuary" of heaven.[3]

For a third example of this idea expressed clearly in Scripture see Ephesians 2:18. Here Paul teaches that Christ "came and preached peace to you who were far off and peace to those who were near; for through him we both have access in one Spirit to the Father."

This same vision permeated the writings of the fathers of the church. For example, writing in the early third century, St. Clement of Alexandria presents Christ as the choir leader of the church's worship.[4] Around the same time, Tertullian was writing

---

1. Cf. Brendan Byrne, SJ, "Philippians," in Raymond E. Brown, SS, Joseph A. Fitzmyer, SJ, and Roland E. Murphy, OCarm., eds., *The New Jerome Biblical Commentary* (Englewood Cliffs, NJ: Prentice Hall, 1990), 795.

2. Cf. Myles M. Bourke, "The Epistle to the Hebrews," in ibid., 921.

3. Cyprian Vagaggini, OSB, *Theological Dimensions of the Liturgy*, tr. Leonard J. Doyle and W. A. Jurgens (Collegeville, MN: Liturgical Press, 1976), 254–59. Cf. Geoffrey Wainwright, *Doxology: The Praise of God in Worship, Doctrine, and Life* (New York: Oxford University Press, 1980), 62.

4. Ibid., 64 n. 153.

of Christ as the *catholicus Patris sacerdos*, "the catholic priest of the Father."[5] And in fourth-century Africa, St. Augustine, speaking of Christian prayer in general, wrote, "He prays for us as our Priest; He prays in us as our Head; He is prayed to by us as our God. Let us recognize our voice in Him, therefore, and His voice in us."[6]

We can see this thinking reflected in just about any liturgy from any period of the church's history, both East and West. It's there from the start, just as clearly as it is in Scripture and the Fathers—which shouldn't surprise us, since the church's liturgical life came before and helped form both the New Testament *and* the Fathers. Though there are a few exceptions, the nearly unwavering norm is that all liturgical prayer is addressed through Christ to the Father.

And so today's *Catechism of the Catholic Church* is on very firm ground when it teaches that Christ "presides invisibly over every Eucharistic celebration" (1348). But he does not do it by himself.

In Persona Christi Capitis

Christ may preside invisibly over every Eucharist, but we humans need something a little more tangible than that (which is, after all, what sacraments are all about). Catholic faith and tradition accord a unique and irreplaceable liturgical role to the ordained priesthood. The priest is the sacramental representation of the ministry of Christ the Priest in our midst.

This is the not the fanciful development of medieval Christian leaders living in a clericalized era, more interested in hierarchy than holiness, far removed from the church's simpler, more scriptural roots. We see it already in St. Ignatius of Antioch, who wrote around the time the Gospel of John was composed. The letters Ignatius wrote to several Christian communities as he was literally on his way to his martyrdom are a fascinating window into early Christian faith and living. To the Magnesians, where it

---

5. *Theological Dimensions of the Liturgy*, 266.
6. Ibid., 265.

seems there was a group of believers who had separated themselves from the Christian community, Ignatius wrote, "The meetings they [those who gather apart from the bishop] hold can have
no sort of valid authority." Similarly, to the community in Smyrna,
he wrote: "The sole Eucharist you should consider valid is one
that is celebrated by the bishop himself, or by some person au-
thorized by him."[7]

Just over a century later, St. Cyprian of Carthage, another
martyr bishop, articulated marvelously the Catholic understanding of the role of the priest at Mass. For Cyprian, the Mass
corresponds to the Last Supper, and the priest stands in place of
Christ. Enrico Mazza explains Cyprian's theology:

> The priest . . . takes Christ's place and repeats his gestures.
> This is not simply an external correspondence, for, according
> to Cyprian there is a real, even if relative, identity between
> the priest and Christ; the priest can be said to participate in
> Christ. . . . In Cyprian's thinking, the priest is the *typus
> Christi* and fills the role of Christ. At times, Cyprian rewords
> this phrase as *vice Christi*.[8]

Mazza also notes that it is this identification between the priest
and Christ that grounds the connection between the Eucharist
and the Last Supper. "For Cyprian, then, the sacramentality of
the priesthood is the ultimate explanation of the sacramentality
of the Eucharist."[9]

This sacramental understanding of the priesthood developed
through the ages, but it clearly was there from the church's earliest days, and it is among the essentials that must be kept in mind
when thinking about the Eucharist. We see it in the *Catechism*
today, which includes in its description of Mass: "the bread and
wine are brought to the altar; they will be offered by the priest

7. Citations are in Enrico Mazza, *The Celebration of the Eucharist: The Origin
of the Rite and the Development of Its Interpretation*, tr. Matthew J. O'Connell
(Collegeville, MN: Liturgical Press, 1999), 97.

8. Ibid., 126. In n. 40 Mazza writes that the most accurate modern translation
for *typus Christi* would be "sacrament of Christ."

9. Ibid.

in the name of Christ in the Eucharistic sacrifice in which they will become his body and blood" (1350).

The problem is that there came a time when some of the *other* essentials were forgotten or minimized, and in the space where these important ideas had been, the role of the priest grew and took on new proportions. As we'll see below, what was forgotten was that the assembly gathered for Mass also has a role in its celebration, that the Eucharist is their celebration as well. When this happened, our understanding of much that goes on at Mass got all out of whack, like the image in a fun-house mirror that enlarges some parts and diminishes others, and what's left is a grotesque distortion of reality.

"But Also Together with Him"

It's worth pointing out a fact so obvious that it is easily over-looked: the subject pronoun of all eucharistic prayers of Christian liturgical tradition is *we*.[10] (Many contain the occasional and brief exception of private prayers of the priest, but even in these, the *we* is by far dominant.)

Here is another clear fact: almost every eucharistic prayer has some element of dialogue to it. In fact, it's the very first words of most of them.

> [The bishop] shall say, giving thanks:
>> The Lord be with you.
> And all shall say: And with your spirit.
> Up with your hearts.
> We have (them) with the Lord.
> Let us give thanks to the Lord our God.
> It is fitting and right.[11]

Sound familiar? It's the opening of the earliest recorded example of a Christian anaphora, written perhaps as early as the beginning

---

10. Cf. Louis-Marie Chauvet, *The Sacraments: The Word of God at the Mercy of the Body*, tr. Madeleine Beaumont (Collegeville, MN: Liturgical Press, 2001), 31–39.

11. R. C. D. Jasper and G. J. Cuming, *Prayers of the Eucharist: Early and Reformed*, 3d ed. (Collegeville, MN: Liturgical Press, 1990), 34.

of the second century (see chaps. 3 and 14). But there's some version of it at the beginning of most others through the centuries, right up to the eucharistic prayers of the Roman rite today. Just as present, if not more, in the anaphoras through the centuries is the "Amen" of the people at the end of the prayer.

In other words, all eucharistic prayers presume an assembly. To be sure, a priest *can* celebrate Mass without an assembly. But the very oddness of the conversation he has with himself in the preface ("The Lord be with you." "And with your spirit." "Lift up your hearts." . . .) should tell us something important about the assembly.[12]

The ancient Roman Canon, still in use today as Eucharistic Prayer I, leaves no question about who is praying the prayer and making the offering to God. In the text of this prayer that appears in the eighth-century Gelasian Sacramentary, the priest prays: "Be mindful, O Lord . . . of all who stand here present, who offer you this sacrifice of praise" and moments later: "O Lord, we your servants who are your holy people, are remembering the blessed Passion of Christ your Son. . . . And thus we offer to your glorious Majesty, from the gifts which you have given, a pure victim, a holy victim, an unblemished victim, the holy bread of eternal life and the cup of everlasting salvation."[13]

Augustine (who would have been familiar with the Roman Canon) insisted frequently on the importance of all the baptized recognizing themselves to be *sacerdotes*, priests. "Clearly this [word]," he wrote, "does not refer only to the bishops and presbyters who are now distinguished by the name of 'priests' in the Church."[14]

---

12. St. John Chrysostom preached in fourth-century Jerusalem: "The eucharistic prayer is common; the priest does not give thanks alone, but the people with him, for he begins it only after having received the accord of the faithful." Cited in Hervé-Marie Legrand, "The Presidency of the Eucharist According to the Ancient Tradition," in R. Kevin Seasoltz, ed., *Living Bread, Saving Cup: Readings on the Eucharist* (Collegeville, MN: Liturgical Press, 1987), 218.

13. Daniel Sheerin, *The Eucharist* (Wilmington, DE: Michael Glazier, 1986), 369–70. See Chauvet on "the priority of the ecclesial 'we'" (n. 10 above).

14. Also from *City of God*, cited in David Orr, "Educating for the Priesthood of the Faithful," *Worship* 83 (September 2009): 431.

The same understanding is presented by the church's magisterium as well. The Council of Trent, unquestionably protective of orthodox Catholic teaching regarding the Eucharist and priesthood, teaches that the sacrifice of the Mass is "to be offered *by* the Church *through* her priests."[15]

More recently, the Second Vatican Council insisted on recovering the ancient idea of "the common priesthood of the faithful,"[16] or priesthood of all the baptized. The Council's Constitution on the Church (*Lumen Gentium*) teaches that living this common priesthood includes receiving the sacraments, pursuing union with God through prayer, engaging in acts of charity and justice, and proclaiming the Gospel to those around us. But it also insists: "The faithful indeed, by virtue of their royal priesthood, participate in the offering of the Eucharist" (LG 10). *Lumen Gentium* further expands on this participation in the eucharistic offering as a share in the priestly function of "the supreme and eternal priest, Christ Jesus":

> For all their works, prayers and apostolic undertakings, family and married life, daily work, relaxation of mind and body, if they are accomplished in the Spirit—indeed even the hardships of life if patiently borne—all these become spiritual sacrifices acceptable to God through Jesus Christ (cf. [1] Pet 2:5). In the celebration of the Eucharist these may most fittingly be offered to the Father along with the body of the Lord. And so, worshipping everywhere by their holy actions, the laity consecrate the world itself to God. (LG 34)

As we will note in chapter 19, this passage not only insists on a truly priestly role in the celebration of the Eucharist but also challenges us by presuming that we are indeed living out an actively apostolic life.

---

15. Session XXII, Chapter 1, in H. J. Schroder, ed., *Canons and Decrees of the Council of Trent* (Rockford, IL: Tan Books, 1978), 145. Emphasis added.

16. LG 10. Translation from Austin Flannery, OP, *Vatican Council II: The Conciliar and Post Conciliar Documents*, 1988 rev. ed. (Boston: St. Paul Editions, 1987).

The Council's Constitution on the Liturgy (*Sacrosanctum Concilium*) is clear that all those who gather for Mass "[offer] the Immaculate Victim, not only through the hands of the priest but also with him" (SC 48). Elsewhere the same document teaches: "[T]he prayers addressed to God by the priest who presides over the assembly in the person of Christ are said in the name of the entire holy people and of all present" (SC 33).[17]

This idea permeates the *General Instruction of the Roman Missal*,[18] for example, article 78:

> The priest invites the people to lift up their hearts to the Lord in prayer and thanksgiving; he unites the congregation with himself in the prayer that he addresses in the name of the entire community to God the Father through Jesus Christ in the Holy Spirit. Furthermore, the meaning of the Prayer is that the entire congregation of the faithful should join itself with Christ in confessing the great deeds of God and in the offering of Sacrifice. The Eucharistic Prayer demands that all listen to it with reverence and in silence.[19]

In the eternal life of the Trinity, Christ offers himself perfectly and eternally to the Father. He lived this out in his earthly life by offering himself in sacrifice on the cross. In the Eucharist the *totus christus*—the "whole Christ," St. Augustine's term for the church in its union with Christ—offers itself to the Father. The ordained priest who presides in the liturgy is, to borrow an image from Theodore of Mopsuestia, "the tongue [who] offers the prayers

---

17. Cf. *Catechism of the Catholic Church* 1348, 1361, 1368, 1369, and 1407.

18. Significantly, when the second edition of the Roman Missal was published in 1975 the term "celebrant" as applied to the priest was removed from thirty-two passages where it had appeared in the first edition. It was replaced by the term "celebrating priest" or simply "priest." The thinking behind the change was that the priest is not the only one who celebrates the Eucharist, which the term celebrant suggests. See Enrico Mazza, *The Eucharistic Prayers of the Roman Rite*, tr. Matthew J. O'Connell (New York, Pueblo, 1986), 304 n. 108. The term *presider* for the one who leads the eucharistic celebration is an ancient one (cf. Alexander Schmemann, *The Eucharist: Sacrament of the Kingdom*, tr. Paul Kachur [Crestwood, NY: St. Vladimir's Seminary Press, 1988], 15).

19. Cf. articles 32, 33, 35, and 95.

of all." Priest and people do, as Theodore continues, "make the offering in common."[20]

The vocal involvement of the people—in the preface, the Sanctus, the memorial acclamation, and the Amen of the current Roman rite—are *expressions* of the fact that this is a common offering, in which they are involved throughout. Some historical anaphoras have contained fewer moments to express the assembly's participation vocally; others have contained considerably more.[21]

Joseph Ratzinger, now Pope Benedict XVI, puts the matter quite beautifully:

> In sum we can say that neither the priest alone nor the community alone is the celebrant of the liturgy, but the whole Christ is the celebrant, head and members. The priest, the assembly, and the single individuals are all celebrant insofar as they are united with Christ and insofar as they represent him in the communion of head and body. In every liturgical celebration the whole Church—heaven and earth, God and humans—is involved, not just theoretically but in a wholly real manner. The more the celebration is nourished from this knowledge and from this experience, the more concretely will the liturgy become meaningful.[22]

Who prays the eucharistic prayer? The answer to that question is indeed, "The priest does." But the *meaning* of that answer is not as one-dimensional as we might think. The priest is Christ; the priest is also the ordained minister who has a special and unique share in Christ's priesthood and exercises it in the offering of the Mass; the priest is also each of the baptized who gather for Mass, who share too in the priesthood of Jesus Christ and exercise it in offering the eucharistic sacrifice.

---

20. Edward Yarnold, SJ, *The Awe-Inspiring Rites of Initiation: The Origins of the R.C.I.A.*, 2d ed. (Collegeville, MN: Liturgical Press, 1994), 220, 223.

21. For one early anaphora that includes a notable amount of participation by the assembly see the "Anaphora of the Twelve Apostles," the date and origin of which are uncertain: Jasper and Cuming, *Prayers of the Eucharist*, 125–28.

22. Joseph Cardinal Ratzinger, *A New Song for the Lord: Faith in Christ and Liturgy Today*, tr. Martha M. Matesich (New York: Crossroad, 1996), 135.

The History of the Eucharistic Prayer

The church's liturgical life is like the life of a family. Even for members who are unaware of it, what came before constantly forms and determines what is now. What we have in our liturgy we have received from our forebears and through them from the Lord; entrusted with it, we faithfully carry it on in our own day and then pass it on to those who come after us. Historical experience, therefore, is never just an interesting side note when it comes to liturgy.

With that in mind, let's take a quick tour through liturgical history, watching the development of the eucharistic prayer and stopping here and there to take a look at some examples of what it looked like at various points.

Jewish Roots: God's Prep Work

The eucharistic prayer is rooted in the prayer Jesus prayed at the Last Supper. But Jesus was not simply ad-libbing a new and original prayer that evening. He was a faithful Jewish man, and one aspect of the life of every faithful Jew was the prayer known as the *berakah*.[1] Because of the *berakah*'s place in the history and development of the Eucharist, Louis Bouyer called it "providence's preparatory work."[2]

---

1. The singular form of the word is *berakah*. The plural form is *berakoth*.
2. Louis Bouyer, *Eucharist: Theology and Spirituality of the Eucharistic Prayer*, tr. Charles Underhill Quinn (Notre Dame, IN: University of Notre Dame Press, 1968), 16.

Berakoth praise (or "bless") God for the wonderful works God has done. Jews prayed them at important moments throughout their typical day, constantly reminding themselves of God's blessings. Though their specific wording varies, they're easy to recognize, almost always beginning with the phrase, "Blessed are you . . ."[3] (also sometimes rendered in English "I/we give you thanks"). Joy "is the soul of every *berakah*."[4]

The *berakah* is also sacrificial in nature; it developed after the destruction of the temple in Jerusalem and, for Jews in exile, took the place of the sacrificial worship that happened there. When the temple was rebuilt, the faithful who gathered in synagogues prayed their *berakoth* facing the temple. Praying them became "the source of the priestly life of the people of God" and "made the entire life of the Jewish people one priestly action."[5] *Berakah* is a "prayer of offering oneself."[6]

We see the importance of the *berakah* in ancient Jewish life by how frequently it appears in the Bible. In the Old Testament we see it, for example, on the lips of Rebekah (Gen 24:27), Moses' father-in-law Jethro (Exod 18:9-10), David (1 Chr 29:10-22), Solomon (2 Chr 6:3–7:11), and the Levites (Neh 9:5-38). In the New Testament, Jesus prays it often (Matt 11:25; Luke 10:21; John 11:41-43). The thanksgivings with which Paul opens almost every one of his letters reflect his and his audience's familiarity with the *berakah*.

---

3. Most Catholics today will probably be reminded of the two brief prayers prayed at Mass by the priest during the preparation of the gifts, just before the Eucharistic prayer begins:

> "Blessed are you, Lord God of all creation, through your goodness we have this bread to offer, which earth has given and human hands have made. It will become for us the bread of life."
> "Blessed are you, Lord God of all creation, through your goodness we have this wine to offer, fruit of the vine and work of human hands. It will become our spiritual drink."

These are new to the Mass of the 1969 Missal. Those who guided the reform chose to model these prayers on the *berakah* form, though it is somewhat out of place outside the eucharistic prayer itself.

4. Bouyer, *Eucharist*, 93.

5. Ibid., 59, 220.

6. Ibid., 46.

One of the most important *berekoth* of Jewish life was called the *birkat ha-mazon*, the thanksgiving-blessing offered to God at the end of every meal. "Whenever there is a meal bigger than [an olive], the *birkat ha-mazon* is said."[7] The *birkat ha-mazon* gave every meal liturgy a sacrificial tone. For the faithful Jew, after the destruction of the temple "the meal liturgy had the place and significance of the ancient sacrifices."[8]

With this as a background it becomes clear that when we read that Jesus at the Last Supper "said the blessing" over bread and "gave thanks" over a cup (Matt 26:26, 27), these are references to *berakoth*. The evangelists don't even bother to provide the actual words, because they were very familiar to their readers. The only words the evangelists do record are the ones that were novel, the places where what Jesus said represented a startling and unexpected deviation from what the disciples would have expected.

The Early Church:
"He Makes a Lengthy Thanksgiving to God"

The Jewish context within which Jesus celebrated the Last Supper held powerful sway in the life of the first Christians, almost all of whom would have considered themselves Jews as well.[9] The New Testament doesn't provide us with an outline or script from a Eucharist from apostolic times (though many scholars argue that the Last Supper accounts in 1 Corinthians and the gospels, written several decades after the Last Supper actually happened, are influenced by the Eucharist as their authors knew it to be celebrated).

Our first hints about the nature of the early Christian Eucharist outside the New Testament come to us through the ancient

7. Enrico Mazza, *The Celebration of the Eucharist: The Origin of the Rite and the Development of Its Interpretation*, tr. Matthew J. O'Connell (Collegeville, MN: Liturgical Press, 1999), 15.

8. Bouyer, *Eucharist*, 79.

9. Herman Wegman, *Christian Worship in East and West: A Study Guide to Liturgical History*, tr. Gordon W. Lathrop (Collegeville, MN: Liturgical Press, 1990), 5–6, 8–9.

document known as the *Didache*. This is an early example of a genre of Christian writing that came to be known as the *church order*, a collection of regulations regarding morality, liturgy, prayer, and the organization of the Christian community.[10]

The *Didache* was written in Syria during the last half of the first century (the same time the New Testament texts were being composed). It is therefore the earliest of the known church orders. In chapters nine and ten we find these instructions:[11]

> About the thanksgiving, give thanks thus:
> First, about the cup:
>> We give thanks to you, our Father, for the holy vine of your child David, which you made known to us through your child Jesus; glory to you for evermore.
> And about the broken bread:
>> We give thanks to you, our Father, for the life and knowledge which you made known to us through your child Jesus; glory to you for evermore.
>>
>> As this broken bread was scattered over the mountains, and when brought together become one, so let your church be brought together from the ends of the earth into your kingdom; for yours are the glory and the power through Jesus Christ for evermore.
> But let no one eat or drink of your thanksgiving but those who have been baptized in the name of the Lord. For about this also the Lord has said, "Do not give what is holy to the dogs."
> After you have had your fill, give thanks thus:
>> We give thanks to you, holy Father, for your holy Name which you have enshrined in our hearts, and for the knowledge and faith and immortality which you made

10. See Paul F. Bradshaw, *The Search for the Origins of Christian Worship: Sources and Methods for the Study of Early Liturgy* (New York: Oxford University Press, 1992), 80–82; Edward J. Yarnold, SJ, "Church Orders," in Cheslyn Jones et al., *The Study of Liturgy*, rev. Ed. (London: SPCK, 1992), 89–91.

11. Here I follow the translation offered in R. C. D. Jasper and G. J. Cuming, *Prayers of the Eucharist: Early and Reformed*, 3d ed. (Collegeville, MN: Liturgical Press, 1990), 23–24.

known to us through your child Jesus; glory to you for
evermore.

You, almighty Master, created all things for the sake
of your Name, and gave food and drink to mankind for
their enjoyment, that they might give you thanks; but to
us you have granted spiritual food and drink and eternal
life through your child Jesus. Above all we give you
thanks because you are mighty; glory to you for evermore. Amen.

Remember, Lord, your church, to deliver it from all
evil and to perfect it in your love; bring it together from
the four winds, now sanctified, into your kingdom which
you have prepared for it; yours are the power and the
glory for evermore.

May grace come, and may this world pass away.

Hosanna to the God of David.

If any is holy, let him come; if any is not, let him repent.

Marana tha. Amen.

The influence of the Jewish *berakah* is clear here. The intention
is to glorify and give thanks to God for what God had done. We
should point out that this is not intended as a "script" that was
read verbatim by the presider at the Eucharist. In the early centuries of the church the eucharistic prayer was improvised by the
presider, who was expected to articulate certain fundamental ideas
in the prayer. Hence the *Didache*'s conclusion to the above prayer:
"Let the prophets give thanks for as long as they wish."[12]

This is also clear in the writing of St. Justin, who was born in
Samaria, converted from Judaism to Christianity around 130, and
was martyred in Rome around 165. Less than two decades before
his death Justin provided an account of Christian worship in
Rome in his *First Apology*, written to Emperor Antoninus Pius.
He writes:

12. Robert Cabie, *The Eucharist*. The Church at Prayer, vol. 2, tr. Matthew J.
O'Connell (Collegeville, MN: Liturgical Press, 1986), 24; cf. Daniel J. Sheerin, *The
Eucharist* (Wilmington, DE: Michael Glazier, 1986), 354.

> Then bread and a cup of water and mixed wine are brought
> to the president of the brethren, and he, taking them, sends
> up praise and glory to the Father of the universe through
> the name of the Son and of the Holy Spirit, and offers
> thanksgiving at some length that we have been deemed
> worthy to receive these things from him. When he has fin-
> ished the prayers and the thanksgiving, the whole congrega-
> tion present assents, saying, "Amen."

> . . .

> . . . as said before . . . bread is brought, and wine and
> water, and the president similarly sends up prayers and
> thanksgivings to the best of his ability, and the congregation
> assents, saying the Amen. . . .[13]

Again, thanksgiving is the idea most evident, and the prayer is
clearly improvised by the presider.

One more important early witness is worth a look before we
move on. Another early church order is commonly known as the
Apostolic Tradition. Here[14] is the anaphora it presents:

> BISHOP: The Lord be with you.
> PEOPLE: And with your spirit.
> BISHOP: Let us lift up our hearts.
> PEOPLE: We lift them up to the Lord.
> BISHOP: Let us give thanks to the Lord.
> PEOPLE: It is right and proper.

---

13. Justin, *Apol. 1*, 65, 67. Translation by Edward R. Hardie in Cyril C. Rich-
ardson, ed., *Early Christian Fathers*, LCC 1 (New York: Macmillan, 1970).

14. This is the translation provided in Peter C. Cobb, "The *Apostolic Tradition*
of Hippolytus," in Jones, *The Study of Liturgy*, 213–14. This translation more faithfully reflects the prayer's original sentence structure, which I will highlight in
chap. 14. This important and unique structure is not reflected in the translations
in Jasper and Cuming, *Prayers of the Eucharist*, 34–35; Sheerin, *The Eucharist*,
355–56; or Andre Hamman, OFM, ed., *The Mass: Ancient Liturgies and Patristic
Texts*, tr. Thomas Halton (Staten Island, NY: Alba House, 1967), 36–37. The Cobb
version is an English translation of the great scholar Bernard Botte's reconstruc-
tion of the prayer in *La Tradition apostolique. Texte latin, introduction, traduction, et
notes*. Sources chrétiennes 11 (Paris: Cerf, 1946), 12–17.

BISHOP: We give thanks to you, O God, through your beloved Child Jesus Christ whom you have sent us in these
last days as Savior,
Redeemer and Messenger of your plan;
who is your inseparable Word,
through whom you have created all things;
and whom, in your good pleasure, you have sent down
     from heaven into the womb of a virgin;
and who, having been conceived, became incarnate and
     was shown to be your son, born of the Holy Spirit and
     the Virgin;
who, fulfilling your will and acquiring for you a holy
     people, stretched out his hands as he suffered to free
     from suffering those who trust in you;
who, when he was handed over to voluntary suffering,
in order to destroy death and break the chains of the devil,
to tread down hell beneath his feet, to bring out the
     righteous into light,
to set the term and to manifest the resurrection,
taking bread, gave thanks to you and said,
Take, eat; this is my Body which is broken for you;
likewise the cup, saying,
This is my Blood which is shed for you.
When you do this, do it in memory of me.
Mindful, therefore, of his death and resurrection,
we offer you this bread and this cup,
giving thanks to you for accounting us worthy to stand
     before you and to minister to you as priests.
and we ask you to send your Holy Spirit upon the offering
     of holy Church.
In gathering [them] together grant to all those who share in
your holy [mysteries] [so to partake] that they may be filled
with the Holy Spirit for the strengthening of their faith in
truth; in order that we may praise you and glorify you
through your Child Jesus Christ, through whom be to you
glory and honor with the Holy Spirit in holy Church now
and throughout all ages. Amen.

The author of this prayer is clear that what he is offering is a model to follow, not necessarily a text to be read. After presenting his anaphora, he writes:

> And the bishop shall give thanks according to what we said above. It is not at all necessary for him to utter the same words that we said above, as though reciting them from memory, when giving thanks to God; but let each pray according to his ability. If indeed he is able to pray sufficiently and with a solemn prayer, it is good. But if anyone who prays, recites a prayer according to a fixed form, do not prevent him. Only, he must pray what is sound and orthodox.[15]

The fact that the author goes out of his way to emphasize that recitation is not *necessary* suggests that by this time it happened somewhat frequently. We're probably getting a look at a slice of liturgical history that falls in the period of transition between improvised prayers and written texts. It was, after all, the concern expressed by Hippolytus for prayers prayed "sufficiently" and with "sound and orthodox" doctrine that eventually led to normative eucharistic prayer texts.

We'll take a closer look at this prayer in chapter 14. It's enough for now to point out that thanksgiving is the strong theme here, too, though the emphasis on Christ and his death and resurrection is prominent in a way it wasn't in the *Didache*. Also present now is the dialogue introducing the preface and the institution narrative.

These are mere glimpses at the terrain of the early church's anaphoras, but the scarcity of evidence makes them all the more important.

Fourth and Fifth Centuries: Creative Growth

During the fourth and fifth centuries the eucharistic prayer went through a period of striking creative growth. In the East a wide variety of anaphoras were developed, marked by rich

---

15. Jasper and Cuming, *Prayers of the Eucharist*, 36.

theological ideas and evocative language, like a garden whose plants are loaded down with abundant fruits spilling in many directions. Consider, for example, the preface of the Egyptian Anaphora of St. Basil. (Though based on a previously existing prayer, it was probably redacted by Basil himself in the late fourth century.) Following upon the final sentence of the opening dialogue, which is the assembly's response, "It is fitting and right," it reads:

> It is fitting and right, fitting and right, truly it is fitting and right, I AM, truly Lord God, existing before the ages, reigning until the ages; you dwell on high and regard what is low; you made heaven and earth and the sea and all that is in them. Father of our Lord and God and Savior Jesus Christ, through whom you made all things visible and invisible, you sit on the throne of your glory; you are adored by every holy power. Around you stand angels and archangels, principalities and powers, thrones, dominions, and virtues; around you stand the cherubim with many eyes and the seraphim with six wings, forever singing the hymn of glory and saying:

And then the people sing the Sanctus.[16]

It's harder to speak of the early development of Western anaphoras, because we have so few examples to consider. From North Africa, for example, we have nothing from this period. From Milan we have the Canon that is reported by St. Ambrose, clearly borrowed from the Roman liturgy and already looking a lot like what would become the Roman Canon (known today in the Roman rite as Eucharistic Prayer I).

It was during the fourth century that the language of the Roman liturgy changed from Greek, which had been the language of the people, to Latin, which was now the vernacular. There was perhaps almost a century in which people who spoke Latin in their daily lives assembled to hear Greek in their liturgy.

---

16. For other extraordinary examples see the anaphora of the *Apostolic Constitutions* (ibid., 100–13), the Byzantine Anaphora of St. Basil (ibid., 114–23), and the Liturgy of St. John Chrysostom (ibid., 129–34).

Admittedly, the Latin that came to be used in the liturgy was not the same as what was spoken commonly; it was stylized and distinctive, almost a foreign language.[17] The fourth century was also the period in which improvisation was abandoned once and for all, replaced by fixed formulas. If the Eastern anaphoras were a sumptuous garden, the Western prayers were far more reserved and succinct, with less ebullience and emotion.

The Middle Ages: The Silent Canon

Though there were major and dramatic developments in the Roman liturgy in the centuries that followed, the eucharistic prayer remained steadfast in the midst of it all. The words of the Roman Canon barely changed, but the manner in which it was prayed certainly did.

The influence of cultures outside of Rome probably provided the impetus that led to the priest praying the Canon in a whisper that was inaudible to the assembly. This happened around the end of the ninth century in Frankish territory (a little earlier in the East), as an expression of the sacredness of its words. Ordo V, a handbook for German priests written just before 900, includes the instruction, then a novelty, that the Canon be recited "in a low voice."[18] The same practice reached Rome and was established there within a century.

By this time the people were not only unable to hear the prayer prayed; they were also unable to see the activity at the altar as it was prayed, because in most cases the altar was against the back wall of the church and the priest faced in the same direction as the people, his back toward them and in their line of sight to the eucharistic elements and vessels. However, exactly when this practice began is no longer as clear as was thought even

---

17. Wegman, *Christian Worship in East and West*, 65–66; Theodor Klauser, *A Short History of the Western Liturgy: An Account and Some Reflections*, 2d ed., tr. John Halliburton (Oxford: Oxford University Press, 1979), 18–22.

18. Cabie, *The Eucharist*, 133; Cyrille Vogel, *Medieval Liturgy: An Introduction to the Sources*, rev. ed., tr. William G. Storey and Niels Krogh Rasmussen, OP (Washington, DC: Pastoral Press, 1986), 161.

recently. Theodor Klauser, writing in 1965, says the practice emerged in the sixth century, though it was only established as a general rule even in Rome around 1000.[19] But many liturgical scholars today acknowledge that Klauser's dating here is off. It seems that a concern for "orientation," the priest facing east with the people during the eucharistic prayer as an expression of eschatological expectation, developed much earlier than he suggests. How early is still hard to say, but some have argued that it was practiced in the early church.[20]

The general result of these developments was "a liturgy practiced 'by delegation.'"[21] Rather than the eucharistic prayer being prayed by the assembled church with the bishop as its sacramental head, it was prayed by the priest for the people who stood by as he did.

Another significant development in the West, not in the words of the Canon but in people's understanding of it, was the exclusive emphasis on the words of Christ in the institution narrative. We'll look at this a bit more closely in chapter 7, but suffice it to say here that in the thirteenth century St. Thomas Aquinas was able to write as though these were the only important words in the prayer, the rest being superfluous and devotional.[22]

The combination of this thinking, along with the silent Canon and east-facing priest, and the additional fact that the faithful rarely received Communion, resulted in the thirteenth-century development of the elevation of the host and chalice taking a major place in the praying of the prayer. This emphasized the exact moment of consecration, and also allowed the faithful to at

19. Klauser, *Short History*, 100–1.

20. Alcuin Reid, OSB, *The Organic Development of the Liturgy: The Principles of Liturgical Reform and Their Relation to the Twentieth-Century Liturgical Movement Prior to the Second Vatican Council*, 2d ed. (San Francisco: Ignatius Press, 2005), 102. Cf. Godfrey Diekmann, OSB, "Liturgical Briefs," *Worship* 31 (1956–57): 610ff. (cited by Reid, *Organic Development*); Marcel Metzger, "La Plâce des Liturges a l'Autel," *Revue des Sciences Religieuses* 45 (1971): 113–45; Uwe Michael Lang, *Turning Towards the Lord: Orientation in Liturgical Prayer* (San Francisco: Ignatius Press, 2004); Jaime Lara, "*Versus Populum* Revisited," *Worship* 68 (1994): 210–21.

21. Carol Heitz, cited in Wegman, *Christian Worship in East and West*, 194.

22. Mazza, *Celebration of the Eucharist*, 210.

least look upon the host, since they would not be eating it. By the fourteenth century the elevation was often seen as the pinnacle of the entire celebration. The faithful were even encouraged in some places to remove their shoes at the elevation as Moses had removed his during his encounter with the Lord on Sinai.[23]

In initiating the sixteenth-century Reformation, Martin Luther rejected not only the church's eucharistic doctrines but also its eucharistic prayer. In his liturgical reforms of 1523 and 1526 he eviscerated the eucharistic prayer, leaving little other than the preface and the words of institution. It's ironic that in his desire to reject medieval accretions to the liturgy he ended up throwing out everything except what had taken on disproportionate importance during the Middle Ages, the consecration. What is left is practically no eucharistic prayer at all.[24] The 1542 reforms of John Calvin left even less trace of the eucharistic prayer behind.[25]

The Council of Trent responded in its twenty-second session, in 1562. Its decrees include a firm defense of the Roman Canon, insisting that "the Catholic Church, to the end that it [the sacrifice of the Mass] might be worthily and reverently offered and received, instituted many centuries ago the holy canon, which is so free from error that it contains nothing that does not in the highest degree savor of a certain holiness and piety and raise up to God the minds of those who offer. For it consists partly of the very words of the Lord, partly of the traditions of the Apostles, and also of pious regulations of holy pontiffs."[26]

In this defensive posture Trent did little more than affirm the universality of the Roman Canon in the Roman rite. This was the state of things for the next four hundred years, so that a 1924 book

23. Nathan Mitchell, OSB, *Cult and Controversy: The Worship of the Eucharist Outside Mass* (New York: Pueblo, 1982), 176–84; Wegman, *Christian Worship in East and West*, 230. Elevating the host and adoring during Mass led to the development of the monstrance and prolonged adoration outside of Mass. Later, eucharistic processions with the host in the monstrance were a further development from this (cf. ibid., 230).

24. Mazza, *Celebration of the Eucharist*, 237–41.

25. Ibid., 243–44.

26. H. J. Schroeder, OP, ed., *The Canons and Decrees of the Council of Trent* (Rockford, IL: Tan Books, 1978), 146–47.

called the Roman Canon "a prayer unaltered and unalterable."[27] Through the late 1950s, "to have suggested modest reforms [of the Roman Canon] (such as shortening the lists of saints or eliminating some signs of the cross) was to have approached offending pious ears."[28]

The Twentieth Century: What Was Once Unthinkable

The earliest significant twentieth-century suggestion for any sort of change or development of the Roman Canon seems to have come in 1949 from the well-known scholar Joseph Jungmann, SJ, who proposed that it be reformed and shortened.[29] Participants in a 1951 liturgical conference at Maria Laach Abbey proposed significant revisions of the Roman Canon, but only suggestions for some minor revisions were ultimately included in the conclusions that were drafted at the end of the conference and submitted to the Vatican[30] (which suggests the extraordinary nature of such a proposal at the time). Other proposals for change, some minor and some more significant, followed.[31]

These suggestions did not initially gain wide support or even notice. But the liturgical movement was developing in significant ways. Major works of liturgical history and liturgical theology were being produced, and important efforts were made to make their ideas accessible to laypeople. The official church was responsive to this work, as evidenced in the 1951 reform of the Easter Vigil Mass, the 1955 reform of the Holy Week liturgies, and the 1955 encyclical *Musicae sacrae disciplina*, on sacred music.

27. Ildefonso Schuster, OSB, *The Sacramentary: Historical and Liturgical Notes on the Roman Missal*, vol. 1, tr. Arthur Levelis-Marke (London: Burns, Oates, and Washbourne, 1924), 317 (cited in Reid, *Organic Development*, 194).

28. Aidan Kavanagh, "Thoughts on the New Eucharistic Prayers," *Worship* 43 (1969): 2. In 1964, Louis Bouyer was still writing of "the great eucharistic prayer, which in the Western Tradition remains always and substantially the same" (*The Liturgy Revived: A Doctrinal Commentary of the Conciliar Constitution on the Liturgy* [London: Darton, Longman, and Todd, 1965], 95; quoted by Reid, *Organic Development*, 193).

29. Cf. Reid, *Organic Development*, 170–71, esp. 170 n. 73.

30. Ibid., 191, 193, citing Bernard Botte, who was present.

31. Cf. ibid., 195, 272.

In time the liturgical movement shifted from an effort to help Catholics understand and participate more fully in the liturgy into advocacy for revision of the liturgy itself.[32] The announcement of the convocation of the Second Vatican Council in 1959 introduced widespread expectation of significant changes, in the liturgy and otherwise. As a result, to speak of changing or reforming the Roman Canon was not nearly such a shocking thing in the early 1960s as it had been a decade earlier.

The council promulgated *Sacrosanctum Concilium* on December 4, 1963. By the end of January 1964 the motu proprio *Sacram Liturgiam* announced the establishment of the Commission for the Implementation of the Constitution on the Sacred Liturgy, which would come to be known as the Consilium.[33]

By this time dissatisfaction with the Roman Canon was voiced more commonly among scholars. In 1963 the Swiss theologian Hans Küng (who at the time was serving as a *peritus*, or theological expert, at the Second Vatican Council) published his proposal for a revision of the Roman Canon, which amounted to shortening it. Two years later a German theologian, Karl Amon, proposed somewhat more extensive revisions to the prayer.[34] Many private translations and revisions, as well as newly composed anaphoras (often of lesser quality), began to circulate, and they were sometimes used in the celebration of Mass.[35] (The esteemed scholar Bernard Botte characterized the situation as "anarchy."[36])

32. This shift in the movement's goals is a primary part of the narrative in Reid's *Organic Development*.

33. Ibid., 49–50.

34. These are reprinted in Cipriano Vagaggini, *The Canon of the Mass and Liturgical Reform*, tr. Peter Coughlan (Staten Island, NY: Alba House, 1967), 76–83.

35. Ibid., 465–67. Cf. Robert F. Hoey, ed., *The Experimental Liturgy Book* (New York: Herder and Herder, 1969), for a wide variety of examples of American compositions as well as some English translations of foreign ones.

36. Bernard Botte, *From Silence to Participation: An Insider's View of Liturgical Renewal* (Washington, DC: Pastoral Press, 1988), 147–48. In 1973 the Congregation for Divine Worship found it necessary to insist to the world's bishops that they prevent the use of unapproved eucharistic prayers: "The conferences of bishops and the bishops individually are urgently requested that by using compelling reasons they lead priests to respect the one practice of the Roman Church: this

Especially influential was the 1966 book by Italian liturgical scholar Cipriano Vagaggini, *Il canone della messa e la refoma liturgica* (published in English the following year as *The Canon of the Mass and Liturgical Reform*). Vagaggini noted the merits and the shortcomings of the Roman Canon and concluded that suppressing the Roman Canon was "unthinkable."[37] But he maintained that the defects in the prayer were also undeniable and significant and concluded that "[a]ny attempt to revise the present canon merely by way of rearranging it, cutting it, or simply patching it up, will inevitably lead to an awful mess. . . . The time when the Roman canon was believed to be irreplaceable because it is 'apostolic' or perfect is certainly over. But it is also true that it is impossible to lay hands on it with impunity under the pretext of improving it."[38]

Vagaggini proposed that the Roman Canon be retained and that two further eucharistic prayers be added to the Missal (examples of which he composed and offered in the book, with extended commentary on content, structure, and sources).[39] His proposals would have a powerful influence on the reform of the Roman Missal.

Having received requests from several directions that new eucharistic prayers be composed and approved for use in the Roman Rite,[40] Pope Paul VI granted permission to the Consilium to compose new prayers; they in turn quickly assigned the task to a committee of respected liturgical historians and theologians.[41]

The group chose to compose three: one short and simple, one of medium length, and one containing a somewhat lengthy summary of the entire history of salvation.[42] The ancient anaphora

---

course will be a service to the good of the church itself and to the correct carrying out of the liturgical celebration" (Circular letter *Eucharistiae participationem*, in *Documents on the Liturgy 1963–1979: Conciliar, Papal and Curial Texts* [DOL] [Collegeville, MN: Liturgical Press, 1982], 248).

37. Vagaggini, *Canon of the Mass*, 107.

38. Ibid., 122.

39. Ibid., 122–23, 124–95.

40. Cf. Annibale Bugnini, *The Reform of the Liturgy 1948–1975* (Collegeville, MN: Liturgical Press, 1990), 105–6; 449–50.

41. Ibid., 450 n. 4.

42. Ibid., 452.

from the *Apostolic Tradition* was quickly taken as the basis of one of the prayers, and this ultimately became Eucharistic Prayer II. The anaphoras that had been offered by Vagaggini in his book were important starting points for what became Eucharistic Prayers III and IV.[43]

When the Study Group had finished the preparation of four prayers (II, III, IV, and another based on the Alexandrian anaphora of St. Basil), as well as nine new prefaces, they were sent to Pope Paul VI, who composed a page of his own observations and had the work sent to the Congregation for the Doctrine of the Faith (CDF) and the Congregation of Rites. Both approved, though the CDF directed that consideration of the anaphora of St. Basil be postponed.[44]

The bishops of the world who gathered in Rome for the Ordinary Synod of 1967 were given copies of the new prayers and asked to vote on whether these prayers should be introduced into the Latin liturgy. The vote was strongly affirmative.[45] On October 24, 1967, the proposed new Order of Mass was celebrated experimentally by the bishops of the Synod in the Sistine Chapel. Eucharistic Prayer III was used in this Mass.[46] A few months later, three other experimental Masses took place in the presence of the pope and invited guests, on January 11, 12, and 13, 1968, in the Capella Matilde of the Apostolic Palace. Eucharistic Prayers I, IV, and III were used on these three dates, respectively.[47]

Definitive approval of the new prayers was given on April 27, 1968, and the new texts were promulgated by the Congregation of Rites in a decree of May 23, 1968. Copies of the prayers were sent to the bishops' conferences of the world on June 2, with approval for use beginning on August 15, feast of the Assumption

43. Ibid., 450 n. 4.
44. Ibid., 460–62.
45. Philippe Rouillard, "Chronique: Les travaux du Synode sur la liturgie," *La Maison-Dieu* 93 (1968): 147; cf. Bugnini, *Reform of the Liturgy*, 351, whose figures seem mistaken.
46. Ibid., 348, 463.
47. Ibid., 361–64.

of Mary.[48] After 1,300 years of knowing very little variation in rite, the Roman liturgy had now officially adopted the "very striking novelty" of offering to the celebrant several eucharistic prayers from which to choose at a given Mass.[49] In the 1970 apostolic constitution *Missale Romanum*, promulgating the new Roman Missal, Pope Paul VI acknowledged that "the chief innovation in the reform concerns the eucharistic prayer."[50]

Reception of the prayers was generally enthusiastic, but there was also criticism. Some specialists complained of the way they appeared to be a patchwork of pieces of anaphoras from various times and places.[51] Others noted the signs of the committee process that produced them, such as emphasis on particular theological themes and agendas, unlike most other eucharistic prayers that have arisen more "organically" from the church's liturgical life.[52] Most famously, two prominent Roman cardinals joined a

48. Ibid., 464. Cf. *Documents on the Liturgy*, 608–9 (DOL 241), 612–13 (DOL 243).

49. Geoffrey G. Willis, "The New Eucharistic Prayers: Some Comments," *Heythrop Journal* 12 (1971): 6. Archbishop Piero Marini (who served as secretary to Bugnini at the time of the reform) recently wrote, "The fact that four Eucharistic prayers were approved was consistent with the early Roman liturgy, which actually had used several anaphoras" (*A Challenging Reform: Realizing the Vision of the Liturgical Renewal*, tr. Mark R. Francis, CSV, John R. Page, and Keith F. Pecklers, SJ [Collegeville, MN: Liturgical Press, 2007], 140–41). This statement seems questionable. The presence of more than one anaphora in the early history of the Roman rite—at different places and times—seems, after all, considerably different from the new circumstance of four anaphoras (not to mention others approved soon afterward, for a total today of 13) from which presiders may choose. There is no evidence to suggest that this was ever previously the case in the Roman rite. The Consilium itself called the introduction of the three new eucharistic prayers a "new departure," noting that a variety of anaphoras within the same rite "has always been the course taken by all the Christian churches, the Roman alone excepted" (Guidelines *Au cours des derniers mois*, to assist catechesis on the anaphoras of the Mass, 2 June 1968, in *Documents on the Liturgy*, 616 [DOL 244]).

50. *Documents on the Liturgy*, 459 (DOL 1360).

51. Aidan Kavanagh, "Thoughts on the New Eucharistic Prayers" (first published in *Worship* in January 1969), in R. Kevin Seasoltz, ed., *Living Bread, Saving Cup: Readings on the Eucharist* (Collegeville, MN: Liturgical Press, 1987), 104, 106.

52. Salvatore Marsili and others, eds., *Eucaristia: teologia e storia della celebrazione* (Casale Monferrato: Marietti, 1983), 255 (the comments are Marsili's).

group of theologians in publishing a harshly critical assessment of the reformed Mass within months of its promulgation. Regarding the eucharistic prayers, the group charged that the prayers implicitly denied the church's faith in the Real Presence of Christ in the eucharistic species and that the Mass is presented more as a simple remembering rather than as a sacramental action.[53]

□ □ □

We will look at each of the new eucharistic prayers closely in Part Three. The Consilium chose to construct them with identical structures, which include the following parts: preface, Sanctus, first epiclesis (for consecration of the bread and wine), institution narrative, memorial (anamnesis), offering, second epiclesis (for unity of the church), intercessions (including commemoration of the saints), doxology, and great Amen. In Part Two we will consider the meaning and role of each of these parts.

---

53. Alfredo Cardinal Ottaviani, Antonio Cardinal Bacci, a Group of Roman Theologians, *The Ottaviani Intervention: Short Critical Study of the New Order of Mass*, tr. Father Anthony Cekada (Rockford, IL: Tan Books, 1992), 40–44.

**P
A
R
T**

**T
W
O**

The Parts of the Eucharistic Prayer

The Preface:
It's about Thanksgiving

Sometimes the beginning of a work, like the overture of a symphony, is the key to understanding it. That's certainly the case with the eucharistic prayer.

The eucharistic prayer begins with a familiar dialogue between the celebrant and the people (though the English was tweaked a bit in the recently revised translation, reflecting more closely the Latin original).[1] We find this dialogue in some of the very earliest examples of eucharistic prayer in the history of Christian worship. The one we use today (which is almost word-for-word the one that opens the anaphora of the *Apostolic Tradition*) sounds like this:

Celebrant: The Lord be with you.
People: And with your spirit.
Celebrant: Lift up your hearts.
People: We lift them up to the Lord.
Celebrant: Let us give thanks to the Lord our God.
People: It is right and just.

---

1. The Congregation for Divine Worship's 2001 instruction *Liturgiam Authenticam* explained: "Certain expressions that belong to the heritage of the whole or of a great part of the ancient Church, as well as others that have become part of the general human patrimony, are to be respected by a translation that is as literal as possible, as for example the words of the people's response *Et cum spiritu tuo*, or the expression *mea culpa, mea culpa, mea maxima culpa* in the Act of Penance of the Order of Mass" (n. 56).

Together Toward the Lord

The first words of the prayer make clear that both priest and people are involved in what is going on. This is *our* prayer. Notice, though, that our attention is not on ourselves. After an initial greeting of priest to people and people to priest, we—people *and* priest—raise our hearts and minds together to God. After the words of this dialogue, in fact, the celebrant is not speaking to us, and we're not speaking to him. Together we turn with Christ to the Father. Together we address the Father in Christ.[2]

It has sometimes been easy to criticize the practice of the priest celebrating Mass "with his back to the people," done for many centuries before the reforms that followed the Second Vatican Council. But we should at least acknowledge that this posture provided a clear image of priest and people facing *together toward the Lord.*

Without a doubt there is much value in the priest facing the assembly during the celebration of Mass. But if what we see is a community of people turning its attention on itself, we misunderstand what's going on. Even when we worship in a church of more modern style, where we may assemble in a circle rather than facing forward in straight rows, we mustn't forget that we're not assembled in a circle in order to look at one another, but so that the Lord can be at the center of all that we're doing there.

Always and Everywhere

The opening dialogue teaches us another fundamental thing. Our first purpose, in this celebration of the Eucharist, *is to give thanks.* This shouldn't surprise us, since giving thanks is central to Christian living in general (see, for example, essential aspects of St. Paul's thought and spirituality expressed in Eph 1:3-10, Rom 3:21-26, and Rom 5:1-11). The very word *eucharist* comes from the Greek *eucharistia*, which means thanksgiving. This is the name the early Christians gave to the anaphora, for in this prayer they gave thanks.

2. See chap. 2 n. 12, above.

As the celebrant continues through the preface there can be no doubt about the centrality and importance of thanksgiving. In all the variable prefaces of the Roman Canon and in Eucharistic Prayer II he proclaims to the Father that "we do well always and everywhere to give you thanks through Jesus Christ our Lord." Always and everywhere: that's a lot of giving thanks.

The preface that is particular to Eucharistic Prayer II calls our thanksgiving "truly right and just, our duty and our salvation." Notice the four descriptive words, each progressively stronger. Enrico Mazza explains that we can go so far as to speak of giving thanks as our salvation because the eucharistic prayer embodies our faith; it is "a profession of faith that justifies."[3] In our very act of thanking God in the Eucharist we receive the gift of salvation.

So the most fundamental thing the church has to say to God is "thank you." What is the significance of this? One thing it tells us is that life is, more than anything else, a gift. It's not primarily something we make for ourselves, something we achieve, something we earn or manage to grasp, but something we *receive*. Approaching our prayer with this awareness, both in our weekly celebration of the Eucharist and in our personal prayer, can't help but shape the way we approach our lives, and the people and events that fill them up.

Don't we live in a world in which many around us think of life as a contest? "I have to get as much for myself as I can and keep everyone around me from screwing me out of what I could have." But if I am formed by the Eucharist, I'm called to see life as a gift, freely given by God. And it's not just a gift to me personally, but to each person around me, to each person with whom I share the planet. When so many people around us live out their lives as if they're participants in a cutthroat game of Monopoly, we must see things differently. We must see ourselves (*including* those Monopoly players around us) as children sitting down to a family banquet, receiving the richest blessings from our heavenly Father.

In the Eucharist, the family, the church, says, "thank you."

---

3. Enrico Mazza, *The Eucharistic Prayers of the Roman Rite*, tr. Matthew J. O'Connell (New York: Pueblo, 1986), 160.

Thanks for What?

Of course, most of us could make a long list of things for which we want to thank God (and I'd suggest that making such a list would be a worthwhile spiritual exercise, especially in conjunction with our celebration of the Eucharist). The variable prefaces mentioned above each specify the subject of our thanksgiving, depending on the mystery in the life of Christ or feast being celebrated in a given liturgy.

But the church's eucharistic tradition, from its beginnings right up to today, has emphasized two fundamental gifts of God, two *mirabilia dei*, God's great wonderworks: *creation* and *redemption*.

God never *needed* to create anything. God is being itself, an eternal and perfect exchange of love and life between and among the Father, Son, and Holy Spirit. God didn't create out of boredom! God created in an act of pure goodness, an expression of his own truth, goodness, and beauty on a galactic scale, and a sharing in time of the eternal Trinitarian life and love, putting creatures in a fundamental relationship of communion with God. Creation.

Then, when humanity, whom of all creatures God had created in the divine image and likeness, by our own choice brought disunion and separation not only to our own relationship with God but to God's relationship with all of creation, God acted in history to restore that communion. The eternal God stepped into human history, establishing, first, an initial and preparatory covenant with a particular people, and then, by his Son's death and resurrection, a new and eternal covenant with all of humanity, dissolving the bondage that kept us from God. Redemption.

Although one element of Christian prayer is, and surely must be, pure praise and adoration of God for who he is in himself, our tradition has almost always been far more preoccupied with offering thanksgiving to God for what he has done. It is for these acts, creation and redemption, more than anything else that we thank him, as a community of faith called into covenant with him and as individual believers made party to that covenant through baptism into Christ. And it is in the Eucharist, more than in any other way, that we do it.

Not an "Introduction"

When we hear the word "preface" we tend to think of an introduction, something not really a part of the thing itself. Many people skip a book's preface or introduction, and they rarely miss much when they do (except of course in the case of this book!). But that is not the case with the eucharistic prayer. The preface is not a negligible introduction at all but an essential aspect of the entire prayer.[4] Remember that, in its earliest days, thanksgiving gave the prayer its very name. That thanksgiving was concentrated in the preface.

One of the distinctive features of the Roman rite has been its rich variety of variable prefaces. The sixth-century Leonine Sacramentary includes over 200 prefaces, but by the eleventh century this number had been reduced to nine.[5]

Around the eighth century the idea that the Canon began with the words following the Sanctus appeared. This was expressed visually in missals through calligraphy and illustrations that separated the preface from the rest of the prayer. The centrality of thanksgiving in the eucharistic prayer receded and other ideas became more prominent and were given greater importance.[6] In the East the epiclesis, or calling on the Father to send the Spirit, was emphasized. In the West the institution narrative (with its "words of consecration") and the idea of offering came to the fore. This was so much the case that the great Roman Canon, the only eucharistic prayer used in the Roman rite for centuries until rather recently, had almost completely lost any explicit mention of giving thanks.[7]

4. Why this part of the prayer even came to be called "preface" in the first place is not entirely clear (see Mazza, *Eucharistic Prayers*, 36–41), but it is likely that the *prae-* of the Latin *praefatio* refers to something done *in front of* someone/something, rather than chronologically *before* something else.

5. Aidan Kavanagh, "Thoughts on the Roman Anaphora," in R. Kevin Seasoltz, ed., *Living Bread, Saving Cup: Readings on the Eucharist* (Collegeville, MN: Liturgical Press, 1987), 53.

6. Adolf Adam, *The Eucharistic Celebration: Source and Summit of Faith* (Collegeville, MN: Liturgical Press, 1994), 69.

7. Writing in 1956, the liturgical scholar Joseph Jungmann could say of the Roman Canon: "these two ideas dominate everything else: the Mass is memorial

One of the most valuable gifts of the contemporary liturgical reform has been a restoration to our Eucharist of the idea of thanksgiving. This was achieved through the introduction of the new eucharistic prayers as well as the restoration of a wide variety of variable prefaces. The current Roman Missal includes over eighty of these. We would do well to let the preface, at the very beginning of our eucharistic prayer, be a reminder of what Eucharist, at its heart, is about. What a perfect way to open this most important moment in the church's life, the eucharistic prayer!

---

and the Mass is sacrifice." He went on to note that the memorial element was too often forgotten following the Council of Trent (Joseph A. Jungmann, SJ, *The Eucharistic Prayer: A Study of the Canon of the Mass* [Notre Dame, IN: Fides, 1956], 10).

The Sanctus:
Stepping into Heaven's Front Door

It's a biblical scene for which some master Hollywood special-effects artist could pull out all the stops. Isaiah, the greatest of Israel's prophets, offers an account of the experience that, more than any other, stamped his ministry and defined his life. The Scripture scholars call it his vocation narrative, the justification he offers for presuming to speak to Israel as a messenger of God.[1]

Holy, Holy, Holy!

It comes in chapter 6 of the book of Isaiah, and by that point in the book some justification is in order, because the previous five chapters include some of the prophet's harshest and most dire preaching against Israel and Judah. Isaiah writes of a stunning vision he experienced, the majestic scene of God on a throne, with angels gathered around in adoration:

> "Holy, holy, holy is the LORD of hosts!" they cried one to the other. "All the earth is filled with his glory!" At the sound of that cry, the frame of the door shook and the house was filled with smoke.

1. Cf. Joseph Jensen, OSB, and William H. Irwin, CSB, "Isaiah 1–39" in Raymond E. Brown, SS, Joseph A. Fitzmyer, SJ, and Roland E. Murphy, OCarm, eds., *The New Jerome Biblical Commentary* (Englewood Cliffs, NJ: Prentice Hall, 1990), 234.

> Then I said, "Woe is me, I am doomed! For I am a man of
> unclean lips, living among a people of unclean lips; yet my
> eyes have seen the King, the LORD of hosts!" (Isa 6:1-5)

Attentive readers will see interesting similarities to another
dramatic Bible passage, one written at least eight centuries after
Isaiah. In the book of Revelation the author, John, describes a
series of his own visions, including a dramatic glimpse through
"an open door to heaven" (Rev 4:1) itself! In symbolism that is
characteristic of the apocalyptic style John is using, he describes
a throne in heaven, "and on the throne sat one whose appearance
sparkled like jasper and carnelian" (4:2-3). Flaming torches burn
before the throne, and a sea of glass like crystal stretches out
before it. Rather than speaking of angels, John describes strange
animal-like creatures gathered before God's throne.

> Day and night they do not stop exclaiming:
>   "Holy, holy, holy is the Lord God almighty,
>   who was, and who is, and who is to come." (Rev 4:6-8)

These cries, common to Isaiah's angels and John's celestial creatures, have found an important and prominent place in the eucharistic prayer, in the section known as the Sanctus (the Latin
word for "holy").

With All the Choirs of Angels

As the eucharistic prayer's preface comes to a close, the presider invokes the angels of heaven, making some dramatic claims
about what we're doing at Mass. These introductions vary with
the many optional prefaces in the Roman Rite. One that is common to many of them reads:

> And so, with all the choirs of angels in heaven
> We proclaim your glory
> And join in their unending hymn of praise:[2]

2. This is in the Preface for Advent I, Advent II, and Christmas I, among
others. (Note: these translations may change with the new ICEL translations.)

Eucharistic Prayer IV is notable for its extended attention to the angels in the introduction to the Sanctus. But even that one seems sparse compared to the wording in the Roman Canon prior to the 1969 reform:

> Through the same Christ the Angels acclaim your majesty,
> the Dominations adore you,
> the Powers worship in awe.
> Through him also the heavens and the Virtues of heaven
> join the blessed Seraphim
> in one grand chorus of joyous praise.
> We beg you, let our voices blend with theirs,
> as in humble praise we say:[3]

Of course, this was read quietly in Latin. How much stronger might our sense of the angels—their reality, their activity, and especially their involvement in our celebration of the Eucharist—be if it had been retained in its fullness once the eucharistic prayer was heard by Catholics, Sunday after Sunday, in the vernacular?

Still, the Roman Canon seems almost anemic in its recognition of the angels compared to some of what we find in the Eastern traditions. One of the most notable is from the preface of the Egyptian Anaphora of St. Mark:

> Beside you stand thousands of thousands and myriads and myriads of armies of holy angels and archangels. Beside you stand your two most honorable living creatures, the cherubim with many eyes and the seraphim with six wings, "which cover their faces with two wings, and their feet with two, and fly with two"; and they cry out to one another with unwearying mouths and never-silent doxologies, singing, proclaiming, praising, crying, and saying the triumphal and thrice-holy hymn to your magnificent glory: Holy, holy, holy, Lord of Sabaoth; heaven and earth are full of your glory. Everything at all times hallows you, but with all that

---

3. Preface for Weekdays. The English translation is from the *Daily Missal of the Mystical Body* (New York: P. J. Kenedy & Sons, 1961), 701.

> hallow you receive also, Lord and Master, our hallowing,
> as with them we hymn you and say:[4]

Whatever their differences, all of these introductions remind the assembly that in what we are about to sing we join our voices to those of the angels in heaven, singing before God's throne. The assembly and presider then sing[5] the Sanctus together:

> Holy, holy, holy Lord God of hosts,
> Heaven and earth are full of your glory.
> Hosanna in the highest.
> Blessed is he who comes in the name of the Lord.
> Hosanna in the highest.

The angels' words from the visions of Isaiah and John remind us: When we gather to celebrate the Eucharist we do it in union with the liturgy of praise and offering to God that goes on eternally and perfectly before God's throne in heaven.

The Eschatological Gathering of the People of God

While the Eucharist is certainly about remembering the past (Christ's suffering and dying and rising) and about making the power and grace of that event present here and now, *the lesson of the Sanctus is that it is also stepping into the future, a foreshadowing and initial experience of the ultimate goal of the church and of every Christian: heavenly glory.*

John was able to peer through the front door of heaven, to witness in a vision the eternal praise of God going on before his throne. But in the church's celebration of the Eucharist we step through the door and *join* the angels in their song. As we gather around the altar we are one with them in our praise. In this our Eucharist is already a living image, an initial, sacramental mani-

---

4. R. C. D. Jasper and G. J. Cuming, *Prayers of the Eucharist: Early and Reformed*, 3d ed. (Collegeville, MN: Liturgical Press, 1990), 64.

5. The 1970 *General Instruction for the Roman Missal* indicates that the priest "sings or recites" the Sanctus (55b). In a noteworthy revision, the 2002 edition of GIRM changes this rubric to "sings" (79b).

festation of the experience of heaven. The church gathers around the altar as we will gather around the Lord for all eternity. "[E]very eucharistic celebration sacramentally accomplishes the eschatological gathering of the People of God," Pope Benedict XVI wrote in his apostolic letter on the Eucharist.[6]

"The reason why we utter this praise of God which the seraphim have bequeathed to us," wrote St. Cyril of Jerusalem in the late fourth century, "is that we wish to join the heavenly armies as they sing their hymn."[7] And at the beginning of the fifth century, Theodore of Mopsuestia instructed his faithful that in singing the Sanctus "we should imagine that we are in heaven."[8]

This is stated just as clearly in modern times in the Second Vatican Council's Constitution on the Sacred Liturgy (*Sacrosanctum Concilium*), in a paragraph that is also quoted verbatim in the 1992 *Catechism of the Catholic Church*:

> In the earthly liturgy we share in a foretaste of that heavenly liturgy which is celebrated in the Holy City of Jerusalem toward which we journey as pilgrims, where Christ is sitting at the right hand of God, Minister of the sanctuary and of the true tabernacle. With all the warriors of the heavenly army we sing a hymn of glory to the Lord; venerating the memory of the saints, we hope for some part and fellowship with them; we eagerly await the Savior, our Lord Jesus Christ, until he, our life, shall appear and we too will appear with him in glory.[9]

---

6. *Sacramentum Caritatis: Post-Synodal Apostolic Exhortation on the Eucharist as the Source and Summit of the Church's Life and Mission* (February 22, 2007), 31. See also Pope John Paul II's encyclical *Ecclesia de Eucharistia* (17 April 2003), 19: "The Eucharist is truly a glimpse of heaven appearing on earth. It is a glorious ray of the heavenly Jerusalem which pierces the clouds of our history and lights up our journey."

7. Edward Yarnold, SJ, *The Awe-Inspiring Rites of Initiation: The Origins of the R.C.I.A.*, 2d ed. (Collegeville, MN: Liturgical Press, 1994), 92.

8. Ibid., 213.

9. SC 8, as quoted in *Catechism of the Catholic Church* 1090.

A Song of Adoration

This song we sing, the angels and us, is one of adoration. Isaiah's experience of God was one of transcendence, of *inexpressible otherness*. We see this in the angels' veiling of their faces before God (as both Moses and Elijah did in the Old Testament, as well), in the awe-filled repetitiveness of the word—"Holy, holy, holy!"— and in Isaiah's conviction that he is "doomed" because he has seen God.[10] The angels are not gathered before God in a celestial business meeting or coffee clatch; they are adoring, with their repetitive words of praise serving as fumbling acknowledgment of the glory of God.

If adoration has a place in private prayer (it does), and if it is expressed profoundly in the devotional life of the church through exposition of the Blessed Sacrament (it is), these are only derivative of the corporate adoration that is an essential aspect of the church's liturgical worship.

The Transcendent Lord Is Near Us

We should notice, though, that even to this song of the otherness of God the Christian instinct adds a second element, called the Benedictus. These are words of Psalm 118, which were proclaimed by the citizens of Jerusalem who gathered before Jesus as he entered the town on Palm Sunday: "Blessed is he who comes in the name of the Lord! Hosanna in the highest!" (Mark 11: 9-10; Matt 21:9).

This section was not originally a part of the Sanctus, and there are plenty of examples of early anaphoras that lacked it. The Benedictus was added to the Sanctus in the Roman rite by the seventh century, then by the eighth century in the East.[11]

By a sort of accident of history the two parts became separated for a time in the West and took up two different places in

---

10. Cf. *The New Jerome Biblical Commentary*, 234.

11. Enrico Mazza, *The Eucharistic Prayers of the Roman Rite*, tr. Matthew J. O'Connell (New York: Pueblo, 1986), 285; Joseph A. Jungmann, SJ, *The Eucharistic Prayer: A Study of the Canon of the Mass* (Notre Dame, IN: Fides, 1956), 135.

the Canon. This came as a result of the rich polyphonic compositions into which the Sanctus was set, for performance by a choir,
in the late Middle Ages. These became so long that it became
common for the priest simply to move on into the rest of the
eucharistic prayer, which he prayed quietly anyway, while the
Sanctus was sung. By the time he had prayed the institution narrative the choir had completed the first part of the Sanctus and
it was time for the Benedictus section. Then the 1600 Ceremonial
of Bishops codified this practice, prescribing that the Benedictus
be sung after the consecration was complete.[12] Explanations of
the appropriateness of singing "Blessed is he who comes" to
acknowledge the transubstantiation that had occurred were developed only later, to explain the status quo.

Today, of course, the prayer is back together, and this is appropriate. The church of the incarnate Word does not acknowledge the transcendence of the Lord without at the same time
acknowledging his closeness to us. The same Lord before whom
the angels hide their faces rode the dusty road into Jerusalem on
a donkey.

---

12. Adolf Adam, *The Eucharistic Celebration: Source and Summit of Faith*, tr.
Robert C. Schultz (Collegeville, MN: Liturgical Press, 1994), 75–76; Jungmann,
Eucharistic Prayer, 128, 137. The use of hand bells in the sanctuary has its origin
at least partly in this circumstance. The first bell ringing came before the consecration, as a sign from the altar server (who was the only one who could see that
it was approaching) for the choir to stop singing the Sanctus. See Thomas
O'Loughlin, "Liturgical Evolution and the Fallacy of the Continuing Conse-
quence," in *Worship* 83 (July 2009): 318–20.

The Epiclesis:
The Power Source

Remember that bracing metaphor of Annie Dillard's I mentioned in the Introduction, talking about the lack of understanding most Christians have regarding what we do in our liturgy? "The churches are children playing on the floor with their chemistry sets, making up a batch of TNT to kill a Sunday morning." Turning to the epiclesis, we now remind ourselves of the power source—the bang—that pulses within the eucharistic liturgy: the Holy Spirit.

Epiclesis is a Greek word that means "invocation." In the epiclesis, the presider—and through him, the church gathered to Eucharist—invokes the Holy Spirit.[1] That is, we ask the Father to send the Spirit upon the gifts we offer and upon the church.

To begin, we must point to that *and*: upon the gifts *and* upon the church. Both are part of the church's eucharistic prayer tradition. We don't always find both aspects present in every anaphora,

---

1. Properly speaking, there is such a thing as a non-pneumatological epiclesis—that is, one that does not invoke the Spirit by name (cf. Enrico Mazza, *The Celebration of the Eucharist: The Origin of the Rite and the Development of Its Interpretation*, tr. Matthew J. O'Connell [Collegeville, MN: Liturgical Press, 1999], 144). The Anaphora of Serapion includes two epicleses, but neither one mentions the Holy Spirit; rather, it asks the Father to send the Word upon the gifts. Some argue that the Roman Canon implies an invocation of the Spirit, but it does not explicitly ask the Father to send the Spirit. Interestingly, the 1969 Missal's Eucharistic Prayer for Masses with Children II made no reference to the Holy Spirit in its consecratory epiclesis, but this was "corrected" in the Missal's third edition (2000), with the addition of the phrase "by the power of the Holy Spirit."

and one element is a bit older than the other. Both are found in the eucharistic prayers of the Roman Rite today, though they are divided up and placed separately within the prayers.

In these prayers the first epiclesis comes after the Sanctus and before the institution narrative. Here the priest extends his hands over the gifts of bread and wine on the altar before him and asks the Father to send the Spirit upon them, to change them into the Body and Blood of Jesus Christ. This is the *consecratory epiclesis*.

The second epiclesis comes later, after the anamnesis. Here the presider asks the Father to send the Spirit upon the church to strengthen its communion, or oneness. This is the *epiclesis for unity*.

Let's look briefly at each.

Asking the Father to Send the Spirit to Make Christ Present

The first thing to say about the consecratory epiclesis is that its presence in the anaphoras of the Paul VI Missal is, in historical-structural terms, a bit conspicuous, like someone showing up at a picnic wearing a tuxedo. The composers of the new eucharistic prayers clearly went out of their way to include it in each of the new ones. They added it into the structure of Eucharistic Prayers II and IV, even though their source prayers (the third-century anaphora of the *Apostolic Tradition* for Eucharistic Prayer II and a couple of venerable anaphoras from the Eastern tradition for Eucharistic Prayer IV) did not include it. They included it in the structure of Eucharistic Prayer III as well, even though the closest thing it has to a source prayer, the Roman Canon, does not include a clear one.

Why? To understand, we have to be familiar with a tension that has existed for centuries between Eastern and Western Christianity, related to eucharistic theology and practice. During the Middle Ages the words of consecration took on a dominant place in the Western understanding of the Mass. This moment of the Canon was seen as its "essential" one, without which no consecration of the elements happened and no Body and Blood of Christ became present. All the rest was decoration. At the same time Eastern theology developed differently, emphasizing the epiclesis in a similar way.

Those who composed the new anaphoras seem to have been thinking that an epiclesis after the words of consecration might raise the question of whether the consecration had "happened yet" once the institution account was complete. With the consecratory epiclesis preceding the institution narrative, everyone could agree it had happened by the end of the latter, avoiding such uncomfortable questions.

The interesting thing about this issue is that it has become increasingly clear over the past fifty years that the question about which part of the prayer is more important, or even "essential," can be happily left behind us. Considered in the light of simple historical facts, we find this: neither of the answers provided by the two theological traditions holds up before the data of liturgical history.

It is not difficult to find examples of authentic eucharistic liturgies that lack a consecratory epiclesis. Most ancient liturgies, in fact, had none. On the other hand, though authentic eucharistic liturgies that lack an institution narrative are less common, there are such examples. Liturgies of the past, and even the present, show us that it is possible to have the Eucharist without the "words of consecration."

For some Western Catholics this will sound almost like heresy. A Mass without the consecration? Impossible! In fact, the magisterium of the Roman Catholic Church formally acknowledges that it is possible to validly confect the Eucharist in a liturgy that does not include the words of consecration. We see this in the permission, granted by Pope John Paul II in 2001, for Chaldean Catholics to participate in the liturgy of the Assyrian Church of the East (one of the ancient Eastern Christian churches), though that rite's eucharistic prayer, the ancient Anaphora of Addai and Mari, lacks an institution narrative.[2]

2. Cf. Pontifical Council for the Promotion of Christian Unity, "Guidelines for Admission to the Eucharist between the Chaldean Church and the Assyrian Church of the East." This document is available online at http://www.vatican.va/roman_curia/pontifical_councils/chrstuni/documents/rc_pc_chrstuni_

The lesson here is an important one for anyone who wants to understand the nature of the eucharistic prayer. It is not a particular sentence or phrase of the eucharistic prayer, not a certain set of "magic words," that brings about the wonderful change that is such an important aspect of the Catholic eucharistic liturgy. It is the anaphora as a whole that consecrates.

That's not to say the consecratory epiclesis is not important. In many ancient prayers of liturgical tradition, as in the new eucharistic prayers of the Roman rite, it stands as a witness to the awesome and irreplaceable role of the Holy Spirit in the church's liturgy.

Consider the elaborate and beautiful consecratory epiclesis from the Liturgy of St. Mark, as it was used in Alexandria, Egypt, in the thirteenth century:

> [W]e pray and beseech you, [Lord almighty, heavenly king,] for you are good and love man, send out from your holy height, from your prepared dwelling place, from your unbounded bosom, the Paraclete himself, the Holy Spirit of truth, the Lord, the life-giver, who spoke through the Law and the prophets and the Apostles, who is present everywhere and fills everything, who on his own authority and not as a servant works sanctification on whom he wills, in your good pleasure; single in nature, multiple in operation, the fountain of divine endowments, consubstantial with you, sharing the throne of the kingdom with you and your only-begotten Son, our Lord and God and Savior, Jesus Christ; look upon us and upon these loaves and these cups; send your Holy Spirit to sanctify and perfect them, as almighty God, and make the bread the body and the cup the blood of the new covenant of our Lord and God and Savior and King of all, Jesus Christ.[3]

---

doc_20011025_chiesa-caldea-assira_en.html; also Robert Taft, "Mass without a Consecration? The Historic Agreement on the Eucharist between the Catholic Church and the Assyrian Church of the East Promulgated 26 October 2001," *Worship* 77 (2003): 482–509.

3. R. C. D. Jasper and G. J. Cuming, *Prayers of the Eucharist: Early and Reformed*, 3d ed. (Collegeville, MN, Liturgical Press, 1990), 65–66.

Just as the Spirit made Christ present on earth in his Incarnation and raised Christ from the dead in his glorious resurrection; just as the Spirit gave birth at Pentecost to the church, the body of Christ on earth; just as the Spirit compels and fuels the church's ongoing making-present of Christ through its works of evangelization, charity, and justice—so we witness in the consecratory epiclesis that the Spirit makes Christ present for us, in a sacramental way, in the elements of bread and wine.

The consecratory epiclesis reminds us that the Eucharist is not our work, but God's work in us and for us. It reminds us that what we're involved in here is not magic, but grace.

Asking the Father to Send the Spirit to Make the Church One

But the making present of Christ in the eucharistic elements does not exhaust the work of the Spirit at Mass. From the beginning, the church's Eucharist has been about its unity, and it has always understood the Spirit to have a role in that. Even if the institution narrative and the consecratory epiclesis (both considered in their own way such crucial pieces of the prayer) may be missing at times from various anaphoras, a prayer for the unity of the church almost never is.

As if in imitation of Jesus' Last Supper prayer for the unity of his disciples, this prayer in the anaphora is as constant a part of liturgical tradition as can be found. From the *Didache* ("Remember, Lord, your church . . . bring it together from the four winds")[4] and the *Apostolic Tradition* ("send your Holy Spirit upon the offering of your holy church . . . gathering her into one"),[5] right on up, the epiclesis for unity is there.

This conviction has been a consistent part of the church's doctrinal/theological tradition too—probably *because* it's been ever-present in the liturgical prayers. When we consider Paul's lecture to the Corinthians about their scandalous lack of unity as

4. Ibid., 24.
5. Ibid., 35.

they celebrate the Eucharist, we shouldn't fail to recall that it's coming from one who put thanksgiving at the center of his theological thinking—and yet when it came to the rite whose name meant *thanksgiving*, he wanted to talk about unity![6]

For St. Thomas Aquinas, the *res eucharistiae* is the communion, or unity, of the church. We are made one with Christ, but in the oneness we each share with him, we are made one with each other as well.[7]

Pope John Paul II put it beautifully in our own day, in his final encyclical:

> The gift of Christ and his Spirit which we receive in Eucharistic communion superabundantly fulfils the yearning for fraternal unity deeply rooted in the human heart; at the same time it elevates the experience of fraternity already present in our common sharing at the same Eucharistic table to a degree which far surpasses that of the simple human experience of sharing a meal. . . .
>
> The seeds of disunity, which daily experience shows to be so deeply rooted in humanity as a result of sin, are countered by *the unifying power of the body of Christ*. The Eucharist, precisely by building up the church, creates human community.[8]

The epiclesis, then, is a striking expression of the church's Trinitarian faith, set within its eucharistic liturgy. We call on the Father to send the Holy Spirit, making present the Body of Christ and making *us* the Body of Christ.

6. Mazza, *Celebration of the Eucharist*, 81.
7. *Summa Theologiae* III, q. 73, aa. 2-3.
8. *Ecclesia de Eucharistia* (17 April 2003), 24.

The Institution Narrative:
Real Presence, Sacrifice, Covenant, and Love

Here's a daunting title for a book: *The Holy Sacrifice of the Mass: Dogmatically, Liturgically and Ascetically Explained,* by Rev. Dr. Nicholas Gihr, was originally published in 1877. Weighing in at an even more daunting eight hundred small-print pages, it was an authoritative Catholic theological text for many decades. The copy on my shelf is the "fifteenth impression," printed in 1942.

Over half the book is an exhaustive step-by-step explanation and commentary on the Roman rite Mass. This includes, of course, a long chapter (nearly 150 pages) on the eucharistic prayer, which Gihr calls "the most important part" and "the golden centre of the whole of the Mass liturgy."[1]

Interestingly, Gihr refers to the entire eucharistic prayer, or Canon, as "the Consecration." That's even the title of the full chapter on the Canon. The subheadings of that chapter are:

- ❏ The First Prayer of the Canon before the Consecration
- ❏ The Second Prayer of the Canon before the Consecration
- ❏ The Third Prayer of the Canon before the Consecration
- ❏ The Consecration
- ❏ The First Prayer of the Canon after the Consecration
- ❏ The Second Prayer of the Canon after the Consecration

---

1. Rev. Dr. Nicholas Gihr, *The Holy Sacrifice of the Mass: Dogmatically, Liturgically and Ascetically Explained* (St. Louis: Herder and Herder, 1942), 552.

❏ The Third Prayer of the Canon after the Consecration
❏ The Conclusion of the Canon[2]

The consecration proper—that is, the priest's recitation of Jesus' words over the bread and wine—has given its name to the entire Canon. Also, the whole Canon is presented as a sort of frame for the consecration proper. This approach is not unique to Gihr. Rather, it was the common way of understanding the eucharistic prayer for several centuries.[3]

On Consecration

By the early Middle Ages "the words of consecration" were widely understood in the West to be the singular moment in which the transformation of the elements of bread and wine into the Body and Blood of Jesus Christ actually happened. Everything else in the prayer, and in the entire Mass, was secondary at best.[4]

This position was not (and is not) the official teaching of the church, nor was it the only acceptable theological understanding of the eucharistic prayer. Certainly the Eastern tradition did not share the Western understanding. In explaining the various parts of the eucharistic prayer used in fourth-century Jerusalem, St. Cyril, whose homilies on the Eucharist are an important and theologically rich witness to the early church's eucharistic faith, doesn't even mention the institution narrative.[5] He explicitly

2. Ibid., 16, 552–694.

3. The *Saint Joseph Daily Missal*, a popular mid-twentieth-century missal used by the laity in the United States to help understand Mass better, explained that the eucharistic prayer "enshrines the Sacred Words of the Consecration" (*Saint Joseph Daily Missal* [New York: Catholic Book Publishing Company, 1959], 661). The same missal includes a diagram of the structure of the Mass that labels the entire eucharistic prayer as "The Consecration," as well as including the consecration as one part among the many others in the Canon (ibid., 7).

4. "The consecration," St. Thomas Aquinas wrote, "is accomplished by Christ's words only; but the other words must be added to dispose the people receiving it" (ST III, q. 83, a. 4). Elsewhere he specified that "if the priest were to pronounce only [the words of consecration] with the intention of consecrating this sacrament, the sacrament would be valid," though the priest would be sinning for not observing the church's entire rite (ST III, q. 78, a. 4).

5. Though some (e.g., Edward Yarnold) suggested he intentionally omitted mention of it. Others (including Gregory Dix, E. J. Cutrone, J. R. K. Fenwick, and

points to the epiclesis as the cause of the transformation of the bread and wine.[6] Theodore, the fourth-century bishop of Mopsuestia, is clear about this belief as well: "From this moment [the epiclesis] we believe that they [the bread and wine] are the body and blood of Christ."[7]

But the Western approach took hold there by the time of Thomas Aquinas and dominated liturgical theology and popular piety for the next seven hundred years. It was certainly part of the catechesis I received growing up in a rural Catholic parish in the 1970s.

It's a view worth rethinking. The words of Christ over the bread and wine are clearly not a part of every eucharistic prayer, and may not have been a part of Christian anaphoras from the start.[8] As we noted in the previous chapter, the ancient liturgy of Addai and Mari is a well-known example of this. It is still used by some ancient Eastern Christian Churches, and the Catholic Church formally recognizes the validity of this Eucharist and permits Catholics to participate in it.

That's not to say the words of consecration, or the institution narrative (Last Supper narrative), which is their context, aren't important. They are a crucial aspect of what the eucharistic prayer is all about. But it seems better to see the institution narrative as the consecratory section (or one of them) of an entire prayer that is consecratory in nature. (In the same way, we can say that the epiclesis is the expression or articulation of the epicletic nature of the entire anaphora, or that the doxology is the expression of the doxological nature of the entire anaphora.) Debating epiclesis

---

G. J. Cuming), however, argue that the rite he knew had no institution narrative. See Edward Yarnold, SJ, *The Awe-Inspiring Rites of Initiation: The Origins of the R.C.I.A.*, 2d ed. (Collegeville, MN: Liturgical Press, 1994), 93 n. 14.

6. Ibid., 73, 92.

7. Ibid., 234.

8. Enrico Mazza, surely the greatest living authority on the history and development of the anaphora, is able to wonder when "the account of the Last Supper entered the Eucharistic Prayer," "how and why the account of the Last Supper became part of the anaphora" (*The Celebration of the Eucharist: The Origin of the Rite and the Development of Its Interpretation*, tr. Matthew J. O'Connell [Collegeville, MN: Liturgical Press, 1999], 51, 52).

over institution narrative as the "essential" moment of consecration is like trying to say whether it's mutual respect or self-sacrifice that's "the" key to a healthy marriage.

Of course, precisely how consecration happens is less important than the fact *that* it happens, and in the end we can only adore and give thanks before the truth.

According to Catholic dogma the bread and wine become, at Mass, the Body and Blood of Christ. This faith is expressed in the earliest Christian writings, proposed as dogma by the Council of Trent when the Protestant Reformers rejected it, and reaffirmed repeatedly in modern times, for example by Pope Paul VI in his 1965 encyclical letter *Mysterium Fidei*. That encyclical also repeated Trent's judgment that *transubstantiation* was a particularly apt word for describing this mystery. Of course, there are different ways of understanding, exploring, and explaining these ideas, and some preachers, teachers, theologians, and saints have done better than others at this over the course of centuries. The church's magisterium has helped set boundaries in this task.

Even the use of the word *transubstantiation* (which literally means "change of substance") does not guarantee a correct understanding. There was a famous incident of a theology professor at Rome's Gregorian University in the 1950s who ran afoul of his superiors and the magisterium when he began investigating the substantial change in the elements by studying Communion wafers, both before and after consecration, under a microscope. This might sound odd, but in modern scientific terms a thing's substance refers to its physical components—atoms, molecules, chemical elements—which is exactly what Catholic doctrine insists does not change.[9]

When we speak of the Real Presence, we're talking about Christ's sacramental presence, not a physical presence. "Jesus is not there like a piece of meat. . . . The Lord takes possession of the bread and wine; he lifts them up, as it were, out of the setting of their normal existence into a new order; even if, from a purely

9. Cf. Adolf Adam, *The Eucharistic Celebration: Source and Summit of Faith* (Collegeville, MN: Liturgical Press, 1994), 82.

physical point of view, they remain the same, they have become profoundly different."[10]

We see this clearly in the theology of St. Thomas Aquinas, who insists repeatedly on the importance of understanding the Eucharist in terms of its nature as a sacramental sign (rather than the literal, physical presence of Christ). Asking whether the eucharistic Body of Christ can be seen by the eye, he answers "no," noting that "properly speaking Christ's body, according to the mode of being which it has in this sacrament, is perceptible neither by the sense nor by the imagination, but only by the intellect, which is called the spiritual eye."[11] Bringing up the phenomena of eucharistic miracles that involve bleeding hosts or consecrated wine turning to blood, he concludes that it is not the real, physical body or blood of Christ that is made present in them, though "this is not deception, because it is done [by God] *to represent the truth*, namely, to show by this miraculous apparition that Christ's body and blood are truly in this sacrament."[12] Of course, anyone familiar with St. Thomas's hymns, *Pange Lingua* and *Adore Te Devote*, knows that his theology reflects a rich appreciation and profound love for Christ's eucharistic presence.

As I said, none of this is to suggest the institution narrative is unimportant by any stretch of the imagination. Indeed, I would point to four vital roles it plays in the anaphora.

Witness to the Real Presence

We needn't presume that members of ancient liturgical traditions whose anaphoras do not include institution narratives believe with any less conviction that the bread and wine become the Body and Blood of Christ during the Mass. The same St. Cyril who doesn't mention these words in his step-by-step explanation does have this to say to his people:

10. Joseph Cardinal Ratzinger, *God Is Near Us: The Eucharist, The Heart of Life*, tr. Henry Taylor (San Francisco: Ignatius Press, 2003), 85–86.

11. ST III, q. 76, a. 7.

12. ST III, q. 76, a. 8.

> Do not, then, regard the bread and wine as nothing but
> bread and wine, for they are the body and blood of Christ
> as the Master himself has proclaimed. Though your senses
> suggest this to you, let faith reassure you. Do not judge the
> matter by taste but by faith, which brings you certainty
> without doubting, since you have been found worthy of
> Christ's body and blood.[13]

Still, the speaking of the words of Jesus over the gifts—"This is
my Body. . . This is the chalice of my Blood"—serve as a stark
expression of the church's faith in the Real Presence. This is expressed in the institution narrative's gestures as well as words.
In the present Roman Rite the presider "genuflects in adoration"
before the eucharistic elements after praying the words of institution. The people kneel during the epiclesis and consecration.[14]
(And later, when receiving Communion, they will make a gesture
of reverence. A new specification for the United States in the 2002
GIRM specifies that this gesture of reverence is to be a bow of
the head. The worship of the Eucharist outside of Mass that the
church encourages so assiduously can be seen as an extension of
these gestures of adoration that are part of the liturgy.)

Witness to the Sacrifice

The words of Christ that we hear in the institution narrative
say more than "This is my Body" and "This is the chalice of my
blood." Rather, they speak of his body "which will be given up
for you" and his blood "which will be poured out for you and
for many for the forgiveness of sins." Christ's words over the
bread and wine on the night of the supper pointed forward to
the sacrificial death he was to die the next day, certainly coloring
the meal itself with a sacrificial shade. Repeating the same words
in the context of our rite highlights the sacrificial nature of this
eucharistic memorial of Christ.

13. Yarnold, *Awe-Inspiring Rites of Initiation*, 87.
14. The bishops of the United States have, since 1969, chosen to call for
kneeling from after the Sanctus to the end of the doxology.

In fact, we might take special notice of the statement that his blood will be "poured out for you and for many" (cf. Matt 26:28). In echoing the Suffering Servant songs of the book of Isaiah these words provide particularly strong sacrificial connotations. The Suffering Servant is the subject of a series of songs woven into the book of Isaiah, depicting a faithful servant of God whose unjust suffering at the hands of persecutors expiates the sins of the Israelite people. The most intense imagery of all these songs comes in Isaiah 53, which speaks of the servant who is "pierced for our offenses, crushed for our sins . . . smitten for the sin of his people" and who "gives his life as an offering for sin" (Isa 53:5, 8, 10). Of this chapter John J. Collins writes: "The key notion in chapter 53 is that the sufferings of the righteous can bear the sin of others. This idea is based on the analogy of sacrifice. The logic of the procedure can be illustrated by the famous ritual of the scapegoat in Lev[iticus] 16. Aaron confesses the sin of the Israelites over the goat and puts them on its head, and then it carries the sins off to the wilderness."[15]

By his reference to shedding his own blood for many, Jesus invited parallels to be drawn between his own fate and that of the Suffering Servant.[16] His words in our institution narrative bring out the sacrificial element of the Mass in high relief.

Interestingly, the 1969 reform enhanced the sacrificial tone of the "words of consecration" even more by inserting the phrase "which will be given up for you" into the words over the bread. Though they are a part of Paul's Last Supper account (see 1 Cor 11:24), they had not been included previously in the Roman rite.

Witness to the Covenant

The institution narrative is the anaphora's clearest reminder that when we celebrate the Eucharist we renew the covenant with God that was established in Christ in his paschal mystery. The

15. John J. Collins, "Isaiah," in Dianne Bergant, CSA, and Robert J. Karris, OFM, eds., *The Collegeville Bible Commentary* (Collegeville, MN: Liturgical Press, 1989), 445.

16. Cf. Ratzinger, *God Is Near Us*, 33–34.

words over the cup (identical in all the current eucharistic prayers) make the reference clear: "This is the chalice of my Blood, the Blood of the new and eternal covenant." All four New Testament accounts of Jesus' words over the wine include mention of the covenant: "this is my blood of the covenant" (Matt 16:27-28 and Mark 14:24) or "the new covenant in my blood" (Luke 22:20 and 1 Cor 11:25). It might take modern-day Westerners a little Scripture study to catch the reference there, but if you're a Jewish apostle who has been following the Jewish Jesus, and he says this while sitting at the head of table in a Passover setting, the reference rings out like a klaxon.

The entire story of the Israelite people is one of covenant with God. Through this covenant, which was inaugurated with the blood sacrifice on Sinai and renewed with countless temple sacrifices through the centuries, the Israelites were constituted as the People of God. In referring to a new covenant, then, Jesus is speaking in dramatic language.

One other passage was surely clamoring in the heads of the apostles as Jesus made reference to a new covenant. As I imagine the Supper, I wonder if they sat awestruck as the realization dawned on them that they were living on the cusp of a new moment, long foretold, in the relationship between God and his people. Perhaps one of them whispered to himself these words from Jeremiah 31:

> The days are coming, says the LORD, when I will make a new covenant with the house of Israel and the house of Judah. It will not be like the covenant I made with their fathers the day I took them by the hand to lead them forth from the land of Egypt; for they broke my covenant and I had to show myself their master, says the LORD. But this is the covenant which I will make with the house of Israel after those days, says the LORD. I will place my law within them, and write it upon their hearts; I will be their God, and they shall be my people. No longer will they have need to teach their friends and kinsmen how to know the LORD. All, from least to greatest, shall know me, says the LORD, for I will forgive their evildoing and remember their sin no more. (Jer 31:31-34)

Witness to Love

A final point overlaps with the previous three but is still worth drawing attention to it on its own. The institution narrative provides a compelling image of Christ's love for humanity each time we gather for Eucharist.

"He loved his own in the world and he loved them to the end" (John 13:1). One might expect these compelling words to serve as a fitting introduction to the story of Jesus' crucifixion. Significantly, they appear instead at the beginning of the Last Supper account in the Gospel of John.

Eucharistic Prayer IV repeats John's words about Christ's love almost verbatim in the opening words of its institution narrative. We also find reference to Christ's love at the beginning of the institution narrative of Eucharistic Prayers for Various Needs and Occasions: "On the eve of his passion and death, while at table with those he loved. . . ." Again, in the beginning of the institution narrative of the Eucharistic Prayer for Masses with Children II, we find: "The night before he died, Jesus your Son showed us how much you love us. When he was at supper. . . ."

These anaphoras, like John's gospel, present the Supper as an expression of Jesus' self-giving love. Theodore of Mopsuestia captured this beautifully when he preached, "With a love like that of a natural mother he devised a way to feed us with his own body."

Jesus also provides us, in these words of self-giving and in the actions they point to, with an example of the love his followers are called to. This is reinforced by the fact that in place of the supper narrative presented in the other gospels John chooses to speak of Jesus washing the feet of the disciples. After his act of humble service Jesus says, "If I, therefore, the master and teacher, have washed your feet, you ought to wash one another's feet. I have given you a model to follow, so that as I have done for you, you should also do" (John 13:14-15). Sounds like a slight rephrasing of the command, "do this in memory of me," doesn't it? A few moments later Jesus presents his "new commandment": "love one another. As I have loved you, so you also should love one another" (John 13:34). In the Eucharist, and in particular in the institution narrative, we sit at Christ's school of love.

All four of these ideas—the Real Presence of Christ in the Eucharist, the sacrificial aspect of the Eucharist, the covenant with God that is renewed in the Eucharist, and the love that is revealed in it—find luminous expression in the institution narrative of the anaphora.

The Memorial and Its Acclamation:
The Mass Defines Itself

One of the boldest moves of the revision of the eucharistic prayers after Vatican II was introduction of the *memorial acclamation*, previously nonexistent in Western anaphoras. This new segment was even inserted into the otherwise nearly untouched Roman Canon.

By its placement and its introduction it seems very much like a response to the institution narrative that directly precedes it. But, as its very name suggests, the memorial acclamation is better seen as an anticipation of what follows it, a sort of prefix to the memorial. (Hence one criticism among several that have been leveled at this newcomer to the West's liturgical neighborhood: given its placement in the anaphora, the memorial acclamation has the assembly acclaiming something about the Eucharist before it is mentioned by the presider.)[1]

With this in mind, it seems more helpful to consider first the memorial itself, and only then to take a closer look at the memorial acclamation.

"The Cutting Edge of Salvation History"

A good place to start is with the memorial's very first word: *therefore*. It seems like a humble word, doesn't it? Not a bossy

---

1. See Aidan Kavanagh, "Thoughts on the New Eucharistic Prayers," in R. Kevin Seasoltz, ed., *Living Bread, Saving Cup: Readings on the Eucharist* (Collegeville, MN: Liturgical Press, 1987), 112.

noun or a colorful adjective: it's an adverb, though not nearly as flashy as most others. But, like the turn signal at the front of a car, this little *therefore* does an important job.

There at the beginning of the memorial of every one of the anaphoras in the Missal, *therefore* directly connects this part of the prayer with the words of the presider that directly precede it, that is, with the institution narrative. Jesus said, "Do this in memory of me." *Therefore* here we are, doing it. (Therein lies a strong second criticism: The important connection between the institution narrative and the memorial, summarized in that *therefore*, is blunted, if not completely erased, with the memorial acclamation inserted between the two.)[2]

And what exactly is "this" that we're doing? A crucial question, with a fascinating answer that is easily missed without a little background.

The apostles, having watched Jesus go through a series of familiar meal rituals as they sat around that table in the Upper Room, hearing Jesus say, "Do this in memory of me" (or better: "Do this as my memorial")[3] would have heard more in those words than you or I. All most of us hear, without some explanation of the religious/cultural context, is: "Do what I'm doing here, and do it to help you remember me."

2. It seems very significant that in the Eucharistic Prayers for Masses with Children the memorial acclamation is relocated to a place after the memorial rather than before it. In the Introduction that was published with these two new prayers in 1974, the Sacred Congregation for Divine Worship explained, "This is done for pedagogical reasons. In order that the children may clearly understand the connection between the words of the Lord, *Do this in memory of me*, and the anamnesis by the priest celebrant, the acclamation, whether of memorial or of praise, is not made until after the anamnesis has been recited" (*Documents on the Liturgy 1963-1979: Conciliar, Papal, and Curial Texts* [Collegeville, MN: Liturgical Press, 1982], 633). It seems at least as important that adults understand the same connection. Cf. Enrico Mazza, *The Eucharistic Prayers of the Roman Rite*, tr. Matthew J. O'Connell (New York: Pueblo, 1986), 177.

3. Fritz Chenderlin, *"Do This As My Memorial"* (Rome: Biblical Institute Press, 1982); Joachim Jeremias, *The Eucharistic Words of Jesus*, tr. Norman Perrin (Philadelphia: Fortress Press, 1966), 237–55; Max Thurian, *The Eucharistic Memorial, Part I: The Old Testament*, tr. J. G. Davies (London: Lutterworth Press, 1959), 46.

· But in the ears of the Jewish apostles, from the mouth of the Jewish Jesus, in the context of the Passover setting, the idea of *memorial* (in Hebrew *zikkaron*; in Greek *anamnesis*) carried a lot more meaning—and in some ways, the *opposite* meaning.[4] To us a memorial is a monument to a person or event that is now lost to the past; to the Jewish people a memorial was about a past event being made present again.

It was about remembering God's great saving work on their behalf (freeing them from slavery in Egypt, entering into a covenant with them, leading them to the Promised Land), but with a much more powerful remembering than humans can ever do on their own. The memorial was "an act of collective memory which causes the present to budge."[5] It made past reality present, "telescoping . . . two periods of history, the present and the Exodus."[6] It was sacramental.

We see this idea reflected in Deuteronomy 5:2-3: "The Lord our God made a covenant with us at Horeb. Not with our ancestors did the Lord make this covenant, but with us, who are all of us alive today." We see it, too, in the "this day" of Exodus 13:3-4.

A passage from the Mishnah that speaks of the Passover celebration offers a beautiful illustration of what the memorial was all about.

> It is therefore incumbent on every person, in all ages, that he should consider as though he had personally gone forth from Egypt, as it is said, "and thou shalt explain to thy son in that day, saying, 'this is done because of what the Lord did for me in Egypt'" (Ex 12:27). We are therefore in duty bound to thank, praise, adore, glorify, extol, honor, bless, exalt, and reverence Him who wrought all these miracles for our ancestors and for us; for He brought us forth from bondage to freedom, He changed our sorrow into joy, our mourning into a feast. He led us from darkness into a great

4. W. Jardine Grisbrooke, "Anaphora," in J. G. Davis, ed., *The New Westminster Dictionary of Liturgy and Worship* (Philadelphia: Westminster Press, 1986), 18.

5. Louis-Marie Chauvet, *The Sacraments: The Word of God at the Mercy of the Body*, tr. Madeleine Beaumont (Collegeville, MN, Liturgical Press, 2001), 55.

6. Thurian, *The Eucharistic Memorial, Part I*, 19.

light, and from servitude to redemption—let us therefore
say in His presence, "Hallelujah."[7]

Whether or not the Last Supper was a Passover meal, the
apostles gathered with Jesus in a Passover context,[8] and Jesus
spoke of what they did as a memorial. It must have been shocking, though, to hear him call that meal a memorial *not* of God's
past saving work, but of Jesus himself, and specifically of the
death he was about to experience. To one who saw no significance
in Jesus it would have sounded ridiculously solipsistic. To one
who recognizes Jesus as one sent by God, indeed as God among
us, it might be akin to the president of the United States announc-
ing his abrogation of the old Constitution in favor of a new one
he wants to present to us.

In seeing the Eucharist as a memorial we are saying that it
makes present the saving deeds Christ did for us: his death on
the cross, his resurrection, his ascension into heaven. This makes
our every Mass "the cutting edge of salvation history."[9] In fact,
it takes the concept of Christ's real presence an extraordinary
step further. Rather than simply saying that Jesus' Body and
Blood are present, we are saying even more: *Jesus-living-the-very-
events-through-which-he-saved-us* is made present, and we are living these events in him.[10] The words of the popular Lenten
hymn—"Were you there when they crucified my Lord? Were you
there when he rose up from the grave? Sometimes it causes me
to tremble . . ."—are never so startlingly true as when we are at

7. *The Mishnah*, trans. and ed. Herbert Danby (London: Oxford University
Press, 1933), 150–51. Cited in Aidan Kavanagh, "Thoughts on the Roman
Anaphora," in Seasoltz, *Living Bread, Saving Cup*, 36. More contemporary expres-
sions of the same idea are often found in Seder companions today. Cf. Barbara
Diamond Goldin, *The Passover Journey: A Seder Companion* (New York: Puffin
Books, 1994), 22.

8. Thurian, *The Eucharistic Memorial, Part I*, 21; Enrico Mazza, *The Celebration
of the Eucharist: The Origin of the Rite and the Development of Its Interpretation*, tr.
Matthew J. O'Connell (Collegeville, MN: Liturgical Press, 1999), 25

9. Kavanagh, "Thoughts on the Roman Anaphora," 37.

10. See Max Thurian, *The Eucharistic Memorial, Part I*, 6, and *The Eucharistic
Memorial, Part II: The New Testament*, tr. J. G. Davies (London: Lutterworth Press,
1959), 82.

Mass. "Yes," we answer. Not "we *were* there," but "we *are* there." For here we share in the memorial of our redemption!

It's easy to see, then, that the *therefore* at the beginning of the anaphora's memorial does an important job.[11] The institution narrative concludes with Jesus' words, "Do this in memory of me." And the memorial picks up (after the acclamation), "Therefore, O Lord, as we celebrate the memorial . . ." We state our awareness that we are doing this in obedience to Jesus' command. In this moment, Mazza says, "the Mass defines itself."[12]

It is interesting that the idea of the Eucharist as memorial is strengthened in the new English translations, not only more than was seen in the previous English translations,[13] but even more than it is expressed in the Latin of the Missal's typical edition. Much has been made of the new translations' more literal, rather than interpretive, rendering of the typical edition's Latin. But this is one case in which the new translations are less faithful and more interpretive, providing what Enrico Mazza has called "a theological translation" of the original.[14] Take a look at the chart on page 75.

In the original prayers (as well as in the previous ICEL translation), the idea of anamnesis is expressed as a noun only in Eucharistic Prayer IV. In the other three (including the ancient Roman Canon), the idea comes in a participle, saying that those who offer the eucharistic sacrifice are "mindful" of the Lord's passion, death, and resurrection. The phrase from Eucharistic Prayer IV is

---

11. Curiously, in the previous ICEL translation the memorial's opening *therefore* went untranslated in every case. In the new translation the word is now included. It should be clear with this background information why this seemingly minor change is, from a theological-liturgical point of view, a major improvement. It explains, too, Mazza's strongly worded complaint about "translations which alter [by removing the *therefore*] a liturgical tradition that has always been followed in all the churches (even those separated from Rome by communion) and in all the principal translations into the vernaculars" (*The Eucharistic Prayers*, 75).

12. Mazza, *The Eucharistic Prayers*, 75.

13. See n. 11 above.

14. Mazza, *The Eucharistic Prayers*, 132. Mazza, writing in the mid-1980s, is referring here to the Italian translation of the Roman Missal, which does the same thing with the anamnesis that the new English translations now do.

	Editio typica (typical edition) literal translation	*Previous ICEL* translation	*New ICEL* translation
Eucharistic Prayer I	Therefore, O Lord, we your servants and with us your holy people, calling to mind the blessed passion . . . offer . . .	Father, we celebrate the memory of Christ your Son. We, your people and your ministers, recall his passion . . .	Therefore, O Lord, as we celebrate the memorial of the blessed Passion . . . we, your servants and your holy people, offer . . .
Eucharistic Prayer II	Mindful therefore of his death and resurrection, we offer . . .	In memory of his death and resurrection, we offer . . .	Therefore, as we celebrate the memorial of his Death and Resurrection, we offer . . .
Eucharistic Prayer III	Mindful, therefore, Lord, of the saving passion . . . we offer . . .	Father, calling to mind the death your Son endured for our salvation . . . we offer . . .	Therefore, O Lord, as we celebrate the memorial of the saving Passion . . . we offer . . .
Eucharistic Prayer IV	Therefore, Lord, celebrating now the memorial of our redemption, we recall the death of Christ . . . and . . . we offer . . .	Father, we now celebrate this memorial of our redemption. We recall Christ's death . . . and . . . we offer . . .	Therefore, O Lord, as we now celebrate the memorial of our redemption, we remember Christ's death . . . and . . . we offer . . .

employed in the other three prayers in the new English translation, though it is not there in the Latin texts. Certainly this does not contradict the typical edition in any way or present ideas that are inconsistent with a sound and Catholic eucharistic theology. Rather, the translators have chosen to make more explicit an idea that is present somewhat more subtly in three of the four prayers.[15]

Proclaiming the Mystery of Faith

The very name of the memorial acclamation makes clear that the intention is for the assembly to proclaim together that we are celebrating the memorial of Christ's saving work. In adding this new element to the anaphora the editors of the 1969 liturgical texts chose to introduce it in a curious way.

The phrase *mysterium fidei* ("the mystery of faith") was transplanted from its place in the Roman Canon's institution narrative, in the words over the cup[16] (where its meaning seems to have long been uncertain),[17] to a new location and role as an introduction to the memorial acclamation. (The old ICEL translation expanded on the Latin to say "Let us proclaim the mystery of faith." The new translation renders it simply "The mystery of faith.") It seems that this innovation was a result of a personal decision of Pope Paul VI himself.[18]

15. Ibid. See also pp. 111–12.
16. The Canon's words over the cup had been:
    FOR THIS IS THE CHALICE OF MY BLOOD,
    OF THE NEW AND EVERLASTING COVENANT;
    THE MYSTERY OF FAITH;
    WHICH SHALL BE SHED FOR YOU
    AND FOR MANY OTHERS
    UNTO THE FORGIVENESS OF SINS.
    (Translation as it appears in *Daily Missal of the Mystical Body*, [New York: P. J. Kenedy & Sons, 1961], 709.)
17. In 1949 Joseph A. Jungmann called the phrase "enigmatic," noting "absolutely no agreement" about its meaning and saying that why it was a part of the words of consecration "cannot readily be ascertained" (Joseph A. Jungmann, SJ, *The Mass of the Roman Rite: Its Origins and Development*, tr. Rev. Francis A. Brunner, CSSR [Westminster, MD: Christian Classics, 1986], 199–201).
18. Mazza, *The Eucharistic Prayers*, 175 n. 147.

Three choices of acclamation follow.[19] Despite the reasonable criticisms already mentioned, it seems fitting that the assembly have an opportunity to add its vocal participation to the anamnetic (memorial) portion of the eucharistic prayer, in much the same way that it joins vocally in the thanksgiving portion (through the preface dialogue), the praise portion (through the Sanctus), and in the concluding Amen.[20] This participation at such a significant moment seems to be the most important value of the memorial acclamation.

A final criticism relates to the fact that the acclamations are addressed to Christ. To interrupt an entire prayer, which is addressed to the Father, in order momentarily to address Christ seems problematic to some.[21] On the other hand, acclamations addressed by the assembly to Christ during the anaphora are far more common throughout the Eastern traditions, despite the rest of the same prayers being addressed to the Father.[22] While the eucharistic prayer is traditionally addressed to the Father, one might argue that acclamations by the assembly within it are traditionally addressed to Christ.

19. A fourth acclamation ("Christ has died, Christ is risen, Christ will come again") was not in the typical edition, but was added in ICEL's English translation. It has been removed in the new ICEL translation.

20. See James Dallen, "The Congregation's Share in the Eucharistic Prayer," in Seasoltz, *Living Bread, Saving Cup*, 121.

21. For example, Adrian Nocent in Salvatore Marsili and others, eds., *Eucaristia: teologia e storia della celebrazione* (Casale Monferrato: Marietti, 1983), 255. Nocent points out that the acclamations could certainly be addressed to the Father instead: "Father, we proclaim the death of your Son, and we await his return in glory" (my translation).

22. Dallen, "The Congregation's Share," 117–19.

The Offering:
Making an Offering of Ourselves

The memorial and offering of the eucharistic prayer are so closely related that they are often presented as one structural element, sometimes referred to as the memorial-offering. We see this expressed in the sentence structure of today's anaphoras of the Roman rite as well as in many others of liturgical tradition; one section flows quickly and fluidly into the next, in the same sentence: "as we celebrate the memorial of our redemption . . . we offer. . . ."[1] This sentence structure reflects an important theological connection between the two parts: "[T]he commemoration [that is, the memorial] moves toward the offering and the offering proceeds from the commemoration. There is an ontological connection between the two: admiration, expressed in the anamnesis, is necessarily followed by imitation, expressed in our offering of ourselves just as Christ offered himself."[2]

But they do express two different ideas: the memorial says we are recalling Christ's Paschal Mystery, his own offering of himself to the Father, while the offering says we are making an oblation of our own eucharistic gifts, in union with his. Because

1. See the table in the previous chapter to note the somewhat different ways this is expressed in the original Latin of each of today's four primary prayers.
2. Enrico Mazza, *The Eucharistic Prayers of the Roman Rite,* tr. Matthew J. O'Connell (New York: Pueblo, 1986), 178. W. Jardine Grisbrooke writes that memorial and offering are typically "inseparably linked by making the former grammatically dependent on and relative to the latter" ("Anaphora," in J. G. Davies, ed., *The New Westminster Dictionary of Liturgy and Worship* [Philadelphia: Westminster Press, 1986], 18).

our Eucharist is a memorial, Jesus' offering of himself to the Father is made present. We are present for this, but we are more than observers of the ritual that makes it happen: we join in the offering. We unite ourselves to this offering and make it our own. We offer it, too, to the Father with Christ.

For this reason, and because the *General Instruction of the Roman Missal* divides them into two (see GIRM 79), I will follow that approach here.

What Are We Offering?

The anaphoras make clear that *we are offering Christ*, "this pure victim, this holy victim, this spotless victim" to the Father (Eucharistic Prayer I). We offer his sacrifice, "this holy and living sacrifice" (Eucharistic Prayer III), "the sacrifice of reconciliation" (Eucharistic Prayer for Masses of Reconciliation II). We offer it in the form of the consecrated elements of bread and wine, "the holy Bread of eternal life and the Chalice of everlasting salvation" (Eucharistic Prayer I), "the Bread of life and the Chalice of salvation" (Eucharistic Prayer II), which are indeed "his Body and Blood" (Eucharistic Prayer IV).

"The Church's intention, however," notes GIRM (echoing the Second Vatican Council), "is that the faithful not only offer this spotless Victim but *also learn to offer themselves*."[3] This recalls Paul's demand that Christians offer themselves "as a living sacrifice" (Rom 12:1; cf. 15:16).

To be sure, this is not expressed as commonly in the anaphoras themselves. It is made explicit in Eucharistic Prayer III, which asks that Christ might "make of us an eternal offering to you." We also find it in the Eucharistic Prayer for Masses of Reconciliation II, in the memorial/offering section, where we ask the Father to "accept us, together with your Son."

St. Augustine expressed this conviction about the Eucharist in the fourth century, when he wrote in his *City of God*: "This is the sacrifice of Christians: we, being many, are one body in Christ.

---

3. GIRM 79-80 (emphasis added).

And this is also the sacrifice which the church continually cele-brates in the sacrament of the altar, known to the faithful, in which the church teaches that it itself is offered in the offering it makes to God."[4]

One well-known passage in the Pastoral Constitution on the Liturgy (*Sacrosanctum Concilium*) teaches that the laity "should not be there [at the celebration of the Eucharist] as strangers or silent spectators." The very same paragraph of that document (already quoted in chapter 2) explains this call by insisting: "Of-fering the immaculate victim, not only through the hands of the priest but also together with him, they [the laity] should learn to offer themselves. Through Christ, the Mediator, they should be drawn day by day into ever more perfect union with God and each other, so that finally God may be all in all" (SC 48).

An important passage from *Lumen Gentium* 34, quoted in chapter 2, also needs repeating here:

> For all their works, prayers and apostolic undertakings, fam-ily and married life, daily work, relaxation of mind and body, if they are accomplished in the Spirit—indeed even the hard-ships of life if patiently borne—all these become spiritual sacrifices acceptable to God through Jesus Christ (cf. [1] Pet 2:5). In the celebration of the Eucharist these may most fit-tingly be offered to the Father along with the body of the Lord. And so, worshipping everywhere by their holy actions, the laity consecrate the world itself to God. (LG 34)

This is the *real* participation the liturgy and the church's mag-isterium are calling us to. It's so much more than simply paying attention to the readings and making our responses at the proper time! (Though when this self-offering is going on internally, the attentiveness and vocal participation often flow much more natu-rally.) This is the remarkable reality that is happening in the pray-ing of the eucharistic prayer, and that is expressed in its offering segment. (It is also expressed well in the presentation of the gifts,

---

4. Cited in Louis-Marie Chauvet, *The Sacraments: The Word of God at the Mercy of the Body*, tr. Madeleine Beaumont (Collegeville, MN: Liturgical Press, 2001), 137.

which immediately precedes and prepares for the eucharistic prayer, an element of the Mass that was restored in the 1969 reform of the liturgy.)

We shouldn't conclude this chapter without a reminder that whatever we offer to God, it is only a return of what he has first given us. We'll consider this at greater length when we look more closely at the Roman Canon, which proclaims that what we offer comes "from the gifts that you [Lord] have given us."

The Intercessions:
There's No Such Thing as a Private Mass

Hot ice. Nonstick glue. Peacekeeper missile. Oxymorons all. Add to the list a phrase that for a time crept into the Catholic liturgical vocabulary: the "private Mass."

The next part of the anaphora we'll consider, the intercessions, tells us that we never come to Mass alone. Even the priest who happens to be celebrating Mass by himself for some reason, or a layperson who finds herself the only one in the pews at a quiet weekday Mass—each brings the whole world with him or her. Like the Old Testament priests who went before the Lord in the temple wearing the ephod and breastplate that bore the names of the tribes of the Israelites, so in the Eucharist, and in particular in the intercessions, we stand before the Lord to intercede for the living and the dead.[1]

Eucharistic Prayer I includes prayer for the church, the pope and bishop, and all who "hand on the catholic and apostolic faith"; a commemoration of the living (including a place for the presider to insert specific names and a pause for the people to silently insert their own), commemoration of the saints, commemoration of the dead. Eucharistic Prayer II includes prayer for the church, the pope, the local bishop, and the clergy; those who have died; and for "us all." Eucharistic Prayer III begins with commemoration of the saints, then offers prayer for the

---

1. The comparison of our Eucharist with the Old Testament ephod and breastplate is Max Thurian's: *The Eucharistic Memorial, Part I: The Old Testament*, tr. J. G. Davies (London: Lutterworth Press, 1959), 57–59.

church, the pope, bishop, clergy, "the entire people you have gained for your own," those gathered at that Eucharist, and finally, for the dead. Eucharistic Prayer IV includes prayer for "all for whom we make this offering," including the pope, bishop, and all bishops and clergy; those present and all the church; those who have died; and "us."

Remember, Lord, Your Church

Prayer for the church has always been a part of the Christian anaphora. It's not surprising, then, that today every one of the eucharistic prayers includes some kind of intercession for the church, though the details vary. In Eucharistic Prayer II we ask: "Remember, Lord, your Church, spread throughout the world, and bring her to the fullness of charity." In Eucharistic Prayer III we pray: "Confirm in faith and charity your pilgrim Church on earth." In the Eucharistic Prayer for Reconciliation II it's: "Father, make your Church throughout the world a sign of unity and an instrument of your peace."

In each of these examples we pray explicitly for the universal church. But also strong in the same anaphoras is the original understanding of the church as the local community of believers. The church in this sense is particularly manifested by those assembled for a given Eucharist. And so in the anaphoras today we intercede for "this family, whom you have summoned before you" (Eucharistic Prayer III) or for "those gathered here before you" (Eucharistic Prayer IV). Eucharistic Prayer I, whose intercessions are more dispersed within the prayer, includes prayer for "all gathered here . . . and all who are dear to them."

Every one of the current eucharistic prayers also specifies the pope, the local bishop (both of whom are named), and also the clergy in the intercessions. This is fitting, because both the pope and the bishop are entrusted with fostering the unity of the church. They are the human, personal face of the unity we share. Dennis Smolarski, SJ, expresses this important reality beautifully:

> Our worldwide unity in Christ is not really based on ideology but ultimately on persons: a local parish united around

its pastor; a local diocese around its bishop; several dioceses with their bishops united with the regional archbishop; in some places, a nation united around its primate or patriarch; and all bishops, primates, and patriarchs in communion with the Bishop of Rome. At every level, there is a communion of people and communion of churches, in the end resulting in a universal communion. It is this personal connectedness of our faith that ultimately reflects the personal way the Lord reached out to the people of his land to heal, to teach, to nourish, and to love.[2]

The *Catechism of the Catholic Church* also draws attention to the presence of the pope's and the bishop's names in the eucharistic prayer: "Since he has the ministry of Peter in the Church, the Pope is associated with every celebration of the Eucharist, wherein he is named as the sign and servant of the unity of the universal Church. . . . The bishop's name is mentioned to signify his presidency over the particular Church, in the midst of his presbyterium and with the assistance of deacons."[3]

One intercession that is *not* common in the anaphoras is a prayer for the entire world and for *all* people. Adolf Adam suggests this is because the intercessions have a different purpose than the prayer of the faithful, among which we often include prayers for the world, government leaders, etc. The intercessions of the eucharistic prayer, however, are an expression of ecclesial communion; for that reason issues or persons outside of that communion would be out of place there.[4]

Still, the intercessions of two of the anaphoras do approach including the whole world and all its people in our prayers. The

2. Dennis C. Smolarski, SJ, *The General Instruction of the Roman Missal 1969–2002* (Collegeville, MN: Liturgical Press, 2003), 63–64. For further helpful reflections on the presence of the names of the pope and bishops, on "why the pope belongs in the eucharistic prayer," cf. Joseph Cardinal Ratzinger, *God Is Near Us: The Eucharist, the Heart of Life,* tr. Henry Taylor (San Francisco: Ignatius Press, 2003), 53, 120.

3. *Catechism of the Catholic Church* 1369.

4. Adolf Adam, *The Eucharistic Celebration: Source and Summit of Faith,* tr. Robert C. Schultz (Collegeville, MN: Liturgical Press, 1994), 88–89.

idea is strongest in Eucharistic Prayer III, where we pray: "May this Sacrifice of our reconciliation, we pray, O Lord, advance the peace and salvation of all the world." In the same prayer, moments later, we ask: "in your compassion, O merciful Father, gather to yourself all your children scattered throughout the earth."

Those outside the visible church also get a mention in Eucharistic Prayer IV, when we pray to the Father for "all who seek you with a sincere heart." The ecclesiology in Vatican II's *Lumen Gentium*, in fact, would suggest that those who fit such a description, though perhaps members of other denominations or even unbaptized, in some mysterious way associate themselves with the church.

In Union with the Saints

The intercessions also include a commemoration of the saints, reminding us that the ecclesial communion we share in the Eucharist reaches far beyond here and now. In Eucharistic Prayers II, III, and IV, the only saint mentioned by name is Mary. (Eucharistic Prayer III also provides a place for the presider to mention the name of the saint of the day or the local patron saint.) Each of them also mentions the apostles as a group, and Eucharistic Prayer III mentions the martyrs as a group as well. Otherwise the saints are commemorated as a whole, in phrases such as that in Eucharistic Prayer II, which invokes "all the Saints who have pleased you throughout the ages."

But Eucharistic Prayer I includes the names of forty-one saints! They come in two groups, the first at the beginning of the prayer and the second later toward the end. We'll take a closer look at these in chapter 13.

For Those Who Have Gone Before Us

"Next we recall those who have gone to rest before us. . . . After that [commemoration of the patriarchs, prophets, apostles, and martyrs], we pray on behalf of the holy fathers and bishops and in general for all amongst us already gone to their rest, for we believe that these souls will obtain the greatest help if we make our prayers for them when the holy and most awesome sacrifice has been set on the altar."[5]

These comments from St. Cyril, the fourth-century bishop of Jerusalem, bear witness to the fact that another important aspect of the intercessions has long been to pray for the dead. The same can be said of the eucharistic prayers we use today. Certainly the saints of heaven don't need our prayers, and if there are any souls in hell they can't be helped by our prayers. In this part of the intercessions we are reminded of our communion with the souls in purgatory, and we offer them the help this communion makes possible.

Eucharistic Prayer I provides a place for a name or names to be mentioned, as well as a moment in which presider and people can pray silently for those who have died. Eucharistic Prayer II includes a special embolism that can be inserted, including a naming of the person, when it is prayed in a Mass for the Dead.

Having prayed for the dead, we have now included in our intercessions those who make up what used to be called the Church Militant (those of us on earth), the Church Suffering (the dead in purgatory), and the Church Triumphant (those in heaven). All of these comprise what St. Augustine called the *totus Christus*, the "whole" Body of Christ. It's through our praying the anaphora, and the Eucharist we receive as a result of it, that these "disparate groups" (to say the least!) receive that wholeness.

5. Cyril of Alexandria, Sermon 5, "The Eucharistic Rite," cited in Edward Yarnold, SJ, *The Awe-Inspiring Rites of Initiation: The Origins of the R.C.I.A,* 2d ed. (Collegeville: Liturgical Press, 1994), 93–94.

The Doxology:
Glory Be!

Doxology—sound like another technical and somewhat intimidating liturgical term? Take heart—it's as simple as one of the first prayers many of us learned as children: *Glory be to the Father and to the Son and to the Holy Spirit, as it was in the beginning, is now, and ever shall be, world without end. Amen.*

A doxology is a prayer that glorifies God. It offers God praise, honor, and adoration. (The word *doxology* literally means "word of praise.") Our doxology rang out near the beginning of the eucharistic prayer as we joined in the Sanctus, the angels' song of glory to God. And now as we reach the prayer's close, we return to doxology. It's a message we saw earlier, but the liturgy insists that we mustn't miss it: This is not about us. It's about God. We assemble in Christ not to admire our in-Christness, but to honor the Father.[1] The Second Vatican Council insisted on it as well: "the sacred liturgy is, above all things, the worship of the divine Majesty" (SC 33). (How many lectures and homilies on "liturgy according to Vatican II" have included a citation of that line? If more had, we might have avoided some of the difficulties of recent decades.)

Drawing the prayer to a close with a doxology is a feature common to almost all the anaphoras throughout Christian history.

---

1. "We go back [in the doxology] to the grand function of all prayer, in which the creature bows before his Creator" (Joseph Jungmann, SJ, *The Mass of the Roman Rite: Its Origins and Development*, vol. 2, tr. Rev. Francis A. Brunner, CSSR [Westminster, MD: Christian Classics, 1986], 264).

Most are trinitarian in nature.[2] Some speak of the Persons of the Trinity, using terminology of equality. For example, the doxology of the Byzantine Liturgy of St. Basil: ". . . and grant us with one mouth and one heart to glorify and hymn your all-honorable and magnificent name, the Father and the Son and the Holy Spirit, now and always and to the ages of ages."[3]

But for most, the words reflect that structure of Christian prayer in general, and the Eucharist in particular, addressed in chapter 2: we pray (and in this case, offer praise) *to* the Father, *through* (and with and in) Christ, *in the unity of* the Holy Spirit. We see it in the doxology of the anaphora in the *Apostolic Constitutions*, dating from the fourth century: "For through him [Christ our King] is due to you all glory, worship, and thanksgiving, and through you and after you to him in the Holy Spirit honor and adoration, now and always and to the ages of ages, unfailing and unending."[4]

As with the words of consecration, the Roman Canon's doxology was put to use in all the new eucharistic prayers of the 1969 reform. The intercessions come to a close, and the presider prays, while elevating the gifts:

> Through him [Christ our Lord], and with him, and in him,
> to you, O God, almighty Father,
> in the unity of the Holy Spirit,
> is all honor and glory,
> for ever and ever.

It's a final, ringing affirmation of the nature of liturgical prayer: our prayer taken up into Christ's prayer, which glorifies the Father.

---

2. The doxology of the Anaphora of Addai and Mari is very beautiful, but it is one example of an anaphora that lacks this trinitarian structure: "[Lord], because of all your wonderful dispensation towards us, with open mouths and uncovered faces we give you thanks and glorify you without ceasing in your Church, which has been redeemed by the precious blood of Christ, offering up praise, honor, thanksgiving and adoration to your living and life-giving name, now and at all times forever and ever" (R. C. D. Jasper and G. J. Cuming, *Prayers of the Eucharist: Early and Reformed*, 3d ed. [Collegeville, MN: Liturgical Press, 1990], 43–44).

3. Ibid., 123.

4. Ibid., 112.

Notice, by the way, that the text does not pray that God may be glorified, as though it would be good if he were. It does not even say that we're giving honor and glory to God, as though he is receiving something from us that he doesn't otherwise have. Rather, in the words of this doxology we are acknowledging that "to [God] . . . is all honor and glory, for ever and ever." By his very nature, all glory is God's. The Old Testament emphasizes not that humanity should glorify God, but that God reveals to humanity the glory that is already his. (Remember, for example, Isaiah's vision.) The appropriate response of humanity is to acknowledge this glory.[5]

In fact, the doxology of the anaphora in the ancient *Apostolic Tradition* reflects this in a unique way, adding an uncommon twist: "[We ask you to send the Holy Spirit] . . . that we may praise and glorify you through your child Jesus Christ; through whom be glory and honor to you, to the Father and the Son, with the Holy Spirit, *in your holy Church*, both now and to the ages of ages. Amen."[6] The addition of the phrase "in your holy Church" is striking. It affirms the church as *the* "place" in which God is glorified and even that acknowledging this glory is part of the very nature of the church.[7]

After the doxology, what could there possibly be left to say? Well, one thing.

---

5. See, for example, Donatien Mollat, "Glory," in Xavier Leon-Dufour, ed., *Dictionary of Biblical Theology*, 2d ed., tr. P. Joseph Cahill, SJ, et al. (Boston: Pauline Books and Media, 1988), 202–5.

6. Jasper and Cuming, *Prayers of the Eucharist*, 35. Emphasis added.

7. Cf. Cyprian Vagaggini, OSB, *Theological Dimensions of the Liturgy*, tr. Leonard A. Doyle and W. A. Jurgens (Collegeville, MN: Liturgical Press, 1976), 220 n. 50.

The Great Amen: Our Signature

The Christians of late-fourth-century Rome must have taken their "Amen" pretty seriously. St. Jerome wrote that the Amens proclaimed by the assemblies he experienced there resounded through the Roman basilicas like thunder from heaven.[1]

Come to think of it, for such a seemingly perfunctory part of the prayer it seems that some of the greatest theologian-saints of the early church understood it to have a prominent role in the Mass. Justin includes the Amen prominently in his description of the celebration of the Eucharist in his First Apology and pauses to explain the meaning of the word.[2] Ambrose does the same thing in his *De mysteriis*.[3] Augustine does, too, describing the Amen as the signature that the assembly signs after the priest has prayed the prayer.[4]

It's tempting to pine wistfully for modern assemblies that put the same kind of energy into their eucharistic praying. So far

---

1. Joseph Jungmann, SJ, *The Mass of the Roman Rite: Its Origins and Development*, vol. 1, tr. Francis A. Brunner, CSSR (Westminster, MD: Christian Classics, 1986), 236.

2. Daniel J. Sheerin, *The Eucharist* (Wilmington, DE: Michael Glazier, 1986), 34–35.

3. Enrico Mazza, *The Celebration of the Eucharist: The Origin of the Rite and the Development of Its Interpretation*, tr. Matthew J. O'Connell (Collegeville, MN: Liturgical Press, 1999), 153.

4. Joseph Jungmann, SJ, *The Mass of the Roman Rite: Its Origins and Development*, vol. 2, tr. Francis A. Brunner, CSSR (Westminster, MD: Christian Classics, 1986), 273.

from being like thunder, our Amens at the close of the eucharistic prayer are sometimes more like a weak breeze. (Given Jerome's well-known temper, I'm not sure I'd want to hear the description of it that he would choose.) But it's tough to get excited about, well, one word. Why would those early Christians be so gung-ho about it?

The fact is, the Amen is probably the most important part of the people's vocal participation. It is certainly "the oldest and most basic form of congregational participation" in the anaphora.[5]

While the other moments of the assembly's vocal singing or speaking express its participation in some particular aspect of the prayer, such as the Sanctus or the memorial acclamation, here we are expressing our acceptance and placing our seal on the whole thing. Our Amen says to God that what the priest has just prayed is indeed our prayer as well, and he has prayed it in our name.[6] That explains why the *Catechism of the Catholic Church*[7] singles out the Amen in particular as a manifestation of the participation of the people at Mass.

Particularly given its significance, it's possible that putting all of that in a single word is "inadequate for our culture."[8] It's difficult to get a sense of the weightiness of a moment that passes in an instant. That's certainly why so many composers, when they put the "Mass parts" to music, repeat the word several times or embellish it with others. It is probably also the reason that in some parishes we find that the congregation joins in the singing of the doxology as well. (We should note that this practice is not permitted by GIRM.)[9] But making ourselves aware of the Amen's meaning is certainly a first step toward getting that heavenly thunder rumbling in our own parish churches today.

5. James Dallen, "The Congregation's Share in the Eucharistic Prayer," in Kevin Seasoltz, ed., *Living Bread, Saving Cup: Readings on the Eucharist* (Collegeville, MN: Liturgical Press, 1987), 121.

6. Cf. Mazza, *Celebration of the Eucharist*, 295.

7. *CCC* 1348.

8. Dallen, "The Congregation's Share," 121.

9. *General Instruction of the Roman Missal*, 236.

The Eucharistic Prayers Today

Eucharistic Prayer I: "Accept This Oblation"

The Roman Canon dominates the history of Western liturgy like a Titan. Laud the decision or resent it, there can be no question that the choice of Pope Paul VI and his collaborators to make the Roman Canon (now known as Eucharistic Prayer I) one option among several others for use in Roman Catholic Masses was epochal.

Consider all the generations of Christian faithful, through so many eras of history and places on the globe, who attended Mass with this prayer as its central core. The number of saintly lay people (from Monica to Thomas More to Dorothy Day), religious (from Benedict to Francis to Edith Stein), and clergy (from Gregory the Great to Isaac Jogues to Oscar Romero) who have led lives of heroic holiness nourished by the Mass with this prayer as its beating heart is awesome.

Of course, we must be careful with our words here. We can't speak very generally of how many of the faithful *prayed with these words* while at Mass, because for many centuries most of the laity didn't understand a word of it. We can't even speak of how many *listened* to the prayer at Mass, because the vast majority of the faithful could not even hear it. One theologian has pointed out that if the faith and devotion of sixteenth-century Christians had been more directly nourished by the Roman Canon, many of the troubling ideas that found rich soil in popular piety and helped lead to the Reformation would probably have choked and died as seedlings. (There would likely have been no question, for example, of "earning salvation" or "buying Masses.")[1]

A Long History

The clearest benchmark of the Roman Canon's early history is St. Ambrose's witness to it around 390, in his book *On the Sacraments*. The eucharistic prayer he presents there is not identical to the Roman Canon in its present form, but it's very close.

Ambrose was the bishop of Milan. He probably brought a copy of the Canon from Rome for use in his cathedral in order to celebrate liturgy as it was celebrated in Rome. It's clear from Ambrose's use of the prayer, and his attitude toward it, that it was not new at the time, but was already considered traditional and normative. So we can push its origins back even farther than 390. Since a practice needed to go back at least two generations in order to be considered traditional, we know the Roman Canon has been around, in almost the same form it has today, for at least sixteen-and-a-half centuries![2] After Ambrose the prayer did undergo some development, but it hasn't changed significantly since the beginning of the seventh century.[3]

The next step in the prayer's history was its dissemination. It was being used in England by the seventh century, then was introduced into Frankish territory, Spain, and Ireland in the centuries that followed. By the twelfth century it was the only eucharistic prayer that was used throughout the Western church.[4] At the middle of the twentieth century that was still the case.

The Roman Canon took on such an esteemed position in Western liturgy that some thought its words came from Christ himself. Even well into the twentieth century almost no one would have dared consider the use of any other prayer in the

1. Kevin Irwin, *Context and Text: Method in Liturgical Theology* (Collegeville, MN: Liturgical Press, 1994), 230 (citing John Jay Hughes).
2. Enrico Mazza, The *Eucharistic Prayers of the Roman Rite*, tr. Matthew J. O'Connell (New York: Pueblo, 1986), 58–59.
3. Ibid., 53.
4. Ibid.

Roman rite. That changed around the middle of the century. The history of that change has already been told in chapter 3.[5]

The Roman Canon has a structure different from that of the newer anaphoras of the Roman rite. It is made up of fifteen parts, commonly identified (except for the preface, which is variable) by their opening words. An overview can help us as we consider its contents.

1. Preface: gives thanks
2. *Sanctus*: praises the holiness of God
3. *Te igitur*: asks for acceptance of our sacrifice (#1), petition for the church
4. *Memento domine*: commemoration of the living (who are gathered here)
5. *Communicantes*: communion with the saints
6. *Hanc igitur*: asks for acceptance of our sacrifice (#2)
7. *Quam oblationem*: asks God to bless and approve offering (#3), making them the Body and Blood of Christ
8. *Qui pridie*: institution narrative, words over bread
9. *Simili modo*: institution narrative, words over cup

[memorial acclamation]

10. *Unde et memores*: memorial
11. *Supra que*: asks for acceptance of our sacrifice (#4)
12. *Supplices*: asks that God's angel take our offering to his altar in heaven
13. *Memento*: for the dead
14. *Nobis quoque*: for the ministers, and communion with the saints
15. *Per quem*: final doxology

5. The changes to the Roman Canon introduced by the Missal of Paul VI in 1969 were: the four conclusions to individual prayers were put in parentheses, making them optional; large portions of the two lists of saints were also made optional with parentheses; the memorial acclamations were introduced; all but one of 25 signs of the cross were eliminated; two kisses of the altar were eliminated (cf. Adolf Adam, *The Eucharistic Celebration: Source and Summit of Faith*, tr. Robert C. Schultz [Collegeville, MN: Liturgical Press, 1994], 70).

Fellowship with the Apostles and Martyrs

One of the most interesting characteristics of Eucharistic Prayer I is its lists of saints. In all, forty-one are named (though in the 1969 reform, recitation of most names was made optional). One of the luminous themes in this prayer, then, is the Communion of Saints. It would be difficult for someone to pray his or her way through this prayer without being vibrantly aware of celebrating Mass in communion with the saints of heaven. The two lists fall near the beginning and the end of the prayer. They reflect the devotions to saints most popular among the Christians of the city of Rome at the time the prayer took its final shape.

The first list comes in the *Communicantes*. Having prayed the preface and the Sanctus, asked God to accept our sacrifice, and prayed for all those gathered and their loved ones, we then acknowledge that our prayer is in communion with "those whose memory we venerate." The list then follows. It includes twenty-six saints altogether: Mary, Joseph, twelve apostles, and twelve martyrs. Judas is not included among the apostles, of course, but it's interesting that his name is replaced not by Matthias who took his place (his name will appear in the second list), but by Paul, who called himself an apostle (1 Cor 1:1). Paul was martyred in Rome and his tomb was and remains there.

St. Joseph's name was not present in the prayer until very recently. It was inserted by edict of Pope John XXIII on December 8, 1962, the closing day of the first session of the Second Vatican Council (which the pope had entrusted to Joseph's patronage).[6]

Among the list of the twelve martyrs we find five popes, one bishop, and two other clerics (Lawrence was a deacon, and uncertain legend suggests that Chrysogonus was part of the clergy of Rome). These are followed by four laymen, the two soldiers John and Paul and the two physicians Cosmas and Damian. All

---

6. St. Joseph was declared Patron of the Universal Church by Pope Pius IX in 1847. This designation was certainly the primary consideration in John XXIII's decisions to entrust the council to his intercession and to include his name in the Canon. On St. Joseph's insertion into the Canon see Francis Filas, SJ, *St. Joseph after Vatican II* (New York: Alba House, 1969), 111–66.

were martyred in Rome except Cyprian, who was bishop of Carthage in northern Africa. He was a friend and supporter of Cornelius and, along with being named together in the Canon, they share a feast day.

The second list comes in the *Nobis quoque*. Toward the end of the Canon we pray for the dead and then for those who celebrate the sacrament, asking for "some share and fellowship with your holy Apostles and Martyrs." The list then follows. It includes fifteen saints, all martyrs: John the Baptist, then seven men and seven women. The first of the three men are New Testament figures. The other four men were all martyred at Rome: Ignatius was the bishop of Antioch who was transported to Rome for his martyrdom; Alexander may refer to the pope or maybe not; Marcellinus and Peter were martyred together, the former a priest, the latter an exorcist.

Of the seven women martyrs, Felicity, Agnes, and Cecilia were from Rome. (Felicity is not the martyr always associated with her companion Perpetua. So while the Perpetua named in the prayer may also be a Roman martyr, the name may have been included at some point because of its association with the other Perpetua.)[7] Agatha and Lucy were both from Sicily, and Anastasia was from Sirmium, an imperial city in what is now Serbia.

In various times and places, names have been added to these lists, often reflecting local devotions. There are early Frankish manuscripts that add Hilary and Martin (two great saints of Gaul), as well as Augustine, Gregory, Jerome, and Benedict. Boniface was added at Fulda (in what is now Germany). One French manuscript from the eleventh century includes twenty-three additional names.[8]

---

7. Joseph Jungmann, SJ, *The Mass of the Roman Rite: Its Origins and Development*, vol. 2, tr. Rev. Francis A. Brunner, CSSR (Westminster, MD: Christian Classics, 1986), 254. Jungmann also makes the worthwhile observation that since we lack any significant biographical information about several of the saints mentioned in the Canon this makes these figures "true representatives of the unknown heroes of the first Christian centuries who, because of their glorious death for Christ, continued to live on in the minds and hearts of men" (256).

8. Ibid., 175–76

Following the reforms of 1969 most of the names in both lists were made optional, apparently out of a concern for brevity. Presiders should at least be aware that using this option involves eliminating most of the names representing laity and all of the women.[9]

We, Your Servants and Your Holy People

In the context of the entire prayer, though, it's clear that these lists do not simply express a concern with the Communion of Saints. Rather, veneration of the saints is *one important aspect of a broader preoccupation with the church.* The Canon has a strong ecclesiological theme to it. The lists of the saints with whom we celebrate the liturgy is one aspect of that, but not the only one.

We see this ecclesiological emphasis in the Roman Canon in six ways:

1. Early in the prayer, the *Te igitur* features an extended intercession for the church, immediately after a request (the first of four in this Canon) for the acceptance of the sacrifice. Asking God to accept our sacrifice, we say that we're offering it for the church "first of all." Here the church is described as "holy" and "catholic." Mazza makes the point that at the time the Roman Canon was formed, the word "catholic" was a reference to doctrinal orthodoxy.[10] The closing lines of the *Te igitur* support the idea that this was indeed of concern to the composer of the prayer.

We then pray for the peace of the church, and ask God to "guard, unite and govern her throughout the whole world." It's interesting that we ask him to do this guarding, uniting, and governing "together with" the pope and the local bishop, "and all those who, holding to the truth, hand on the catholic and apostolic faith." Here God is presented as a sort of coworker with the pope and bishops in guarding, uniting, and governing the

9 Cf. Mary Collins, OSB, *Contemplative Participation:* Sacrosanctum Concilium *Twenty-five Years Later* (Collegeville, MN: Liturgical Press, 1990), 30–31.

10. Mazza, *The Eucharistic Prayers,* 62.

church. Also interesting is the suggestion that those who hand on the faith are involved—with God, the pope, and the bishop—in the guarding, uniting, and governing.

2. The intercession for the living in the *Memento domine* adds to the ecclesiological tone of the prayer as well. It begins with a place for the presider to insert names of people he asks God to remember. As the rubric suggests, the presider generally pauses to allow for a silent prayer.[11] But before the entire Canon was read silently, names of those immediately responsible for the offering of this liturgy were probably recited aloud.[12]

The next few lines continue a sentence that in the Latin of the typical edition is long, somewhat confusing, and difficult in structure. The previous ICEL translation tried to clarify this sentence by breaking it into five sentences and simplifying its content. Though it did not offer a strictly literal translation, it was faithful in meaning and more understandable than the new English one, which passes on the difficulty to English-speaking Massgoers.

Even the new ICEL translation, which rarely departs from a strict rendering of the Latin, finds it necessary to make two sentences of the original one in Latin. But faithfulness to the difficult Latin and its effort to be elegant (which it needs to be) means it's still difficult to understand. For our purposes, let's forget the need for elegance and try to get at what the prayer is really saying. Here is my own translation, slavishly faithful to the Latin, but unadorned:

11. The new translation has omitted "especially those for whom we now pray." Admittedly, this phrase is not in the Latin of the typical edition, but it seems like a helpful prompt to those gathered if the presider is going to pause to pray silently here.

12. The historical background to this insertion of names of the living is complex. See Mazza, *The Eucharistic Prayers*, 64, and Jungmann, *Mass of the Roman Rite*, 159–66. Both Mazza and Jungmann mention Jerome's complaint about what was to him an innovation: "Then comes the public recitation of the names of the offerers; here the celebration that is a ransom for sin turns into a commendation of sinners." (See Mazza, *The Eucharistic Prayers*, 64 n. 56 [though the note number itself is inadvertently omitted in the text]; Jungmann, *Mass of the Roman Rite*, 162.)

Remember the people we name
and everyone standing here present
for whom we offer to you
—or who offer for themselves and those who are theirs—
this sacrifice of praise
for the redemption of their souls,
for the hope of salvation and for their safety;
and who offer their promises to you,
eternal God, living and true.

The tricky part is that set of lines at the heart of it: "for whom we offer to you—or who offer for themselves and those who are theirs—this sacrifice of praise."

It's helpful to know that for many centuries the Canon simply asked God to remember those present "who offer you this sacrifice of praise . . . for themselves and for all their own."[13] The "for whom we offer to you, or . . ." was inserted for the first time in the ninth century and became almost universal by the tenth.[14] Rather than the straightforward statement about those present making offering, an alternative is introduced: the offerers may be present, but if they're not, the celebrant is offering the sacrifice in their place.[15]

Here we see evidence of two developments at a particular point in the prayer's history. First, the priest was understood to be offering the sacrifice on behalf of the people who, by the ninth century, were no longer even within earshot of the activity in the sanctuary. Second, the practice of offering Mass stipends had appeared, which meant that it was now common for a person to "offer a Mass" without actually being present at it.

In its original English translation ICEL attempted to provide clearer and more straightforward wording, still true to the meaning of the prayer: "We offer you this sacrifice of praise for ourselves

13. See the Roman Canon printed in Daniel Sheerin, *The Eucharist* (Wilmington DE: Michael Glazier, 1986), 369, which is a translation of the prayer as it appears in the eighth-century Gelasian Sacramentary.

14. Jungmann, *Mass of the Roman Rite,* 166–67; Mazza, *The Eucharistic Prayers,* 65.

15. Ibid.

and those who are dear to us." In the new ICEL translation the complicated wording and problematic background are reintroduced. Either way, in this section the Roman Canon expresses (though more clearly as it existed before the ninth century) the conviction that it is the local church gathered around its altar and led by its bishop/priest that offers the sacrifice. Indeed, it is this gathering, and this offering together, that *makes it* the local church.[16]

3. We see this idea expressed again, and perhaps more clearly, in the *Hanc igitur*. Here we ask the Lord to accept our oblation, which is "of your whole family."

4. We see it still again, very beautifully, in the *Unde et memores* (the prayer's memorial), in which we pray that it is "we, your servants and your holy people" who "offer . . . this pure victim. . . ." So strong is this passage's expression of the corporate offering of the sacrifice that it leads Enrico Mazza to call the Roman Canon "the model for ecclesiology." Here the distinction between priests and people "is mentioned but simultaneously overcome in this splendid 'we,' which points to a single subject of the celebration in all its parts."[17] Anyone who tries to conceive of the priest being the offerer of the Mass on behalf of the people, as if the people somehow have no role in it, has this phrase from the Roman Canon to contend with.

5. We have seen that the Roman Canon expresses a strong awareness of the communion between the church in heaven and the church on earth. This communion is expressed again, in a unique way, in the *Supplices*. In this prayer we ask God to command that the gifts we offer (just referred to: "this pure victim, this holy victim, this spotless victim, the holy Bread of eternal life and the Chalice of everlasting

16. See SC 42: "[All the faithful] must be convinced that the pre-eminent manifestation of the Church consists in the full active participation of all God's holy people in these liturgical celebrations, especially in the same Eucharist, in a single prayer, at one altar, at which there presides the bishop surrounded by his college of priests and by his ministers."

17. Mazza, *The Eucharistic Prayers*, 76.

salvation") "be borne by the hands of your holy Angel to your altar on high in the sight of your divine majesty." Here we encounter again the idea of our participation in the heavenly liturgy, expressed earlier in the Sanctus. (Note, though, that this line was in the Canon before the Sanctus was included.)[18]

6. Finally, we see still another expression of Eucharistic Prayer I's awareness of the eternal dimensions of the church in its prayers for the dead. The *Memento* provides a place to insert the names of specific people (again, the rubrics suggest it is done in silence), which is followed by a prayer that God grant "all who sleep in Christ a place of refreshment, light and peace."

Accept and Bless These Offerings

Despite its attentiveness to this theme of the church, the Roman Canon is marked even more clearly by the idea of sacrifice. Mazza puts it more strongly: the Canon is "based entirely on the theme of offering and sacrifice."[19] If we take this prayer as a datum of the *lex orandi* there can be no doubt of the sacrificial nature of the Eucharist. The Roman Canon is an important liturgical expression of the church's doctrine that Christ instituted the Eucharist "that He might leave to His beloved spouse the church a visible sacrifice, such as the nature of man requires, whereby that bloody sacrifice once to be accomplished on the cross might be represented, the memory thereof to remain to the end of the world, and its salutary effects applied to the remission of those sins which we daily commit."[20]

18. Ibid., 83.

19. Enrico Mazza, *The Celebration of the Eucharist: The Origin of the Rite and the Development of Its Interpretation*, tr. Matthew J. O'Connell (Collegeville, MN: Liturgical Press, 1999), 270.

20. *Canons and Decrees of the Council of Trent*, tr. H. J. Schroeder, OP (Rockford, IL: Tan Books, 1978), 144–45 (Session 22, September 17, 1562). Cf. GIRM 2; SC 47; LG 3, 28; *Presbyterorum Ordinis* 2, 4, 5; *Catechism of the Catholic Church* 1362–72.

One element that's impossible to miss in Eucharistic Prayer I is that it is unquestionably a prayer *asking God to accept* the sacrifice we offer. We ask him to accept our sacrifice not once, and not twice, but four times during the course of the prayer. It's there early, in the *Te igitur*, then in the *Hanc igitur*, the *Quam oblationem*, and finally, it's strong again in the *Supra que*. Four times in the most dominant anaphora in the history of the Christian faith we humbly ask God to accept our offering. Is it necessary? Is it possible that God might not accept our offering? What makes a prayer "acceptable"?

Mazza's comments on this question are insightful. Inasmuch as it is the offering of Christ to the Father, it will always be infinitely acceptable, of course. But inasmuch as it is our offering too—my own offering—it is limited and imperfect. So what's the criterion for whose offering is acceptable and whose is not? The Roman Canon provides its own answer to that question in its reference to the sacrifices of Abel, Abraham, and Melchizedek. These three figures provide "the classical instances of sacrifices acceptable to God."[21] And if we examine them we find that it's not what these men offered that made their sacrifices acceptable, but the purity of heart with which they offered them. "The three names thus reinforce the idea that divine acceptance of sacrifice does not depend on the logic of the rite but on the quality of the offerer."[22]

Important in this regard is the Roman Canon's description of the Eucharist as "this sacrifice of praise" (in the *Memento domine*). The phrase comes directly from Hebrews 13:15, but it has a deep scriptural background. Psalm 50 is a particularly important reference here:

> "Listen, my people, I will speak;
> 	Israel, I will testify against you;
> 	God, your God, am I.
> Not for your sacrifices do I rebuke you,
> 	nor for your holocausts, set before me daily.

21. Mazza, *The Eucharistic Prayers*, 80.
22. Ibid.

I need no bullock from your house,
    no goats from your fold.
For every animal of the forest is mine,
    beasts by the thousands on my mountains.
I know every bird of the heavens;
    the creatures of the field belong to me . . .
Offer praise as you sacrifice to God;
    fulfill your vows to the Most High.
Then call on me in time of distress;
    I will rescue you, and you shall honor me."

But to the wicked God says:
    "Why do you recite my commandments and profess my
        covenant with your lips?
You hate discipline;
    you cast my words behind you!
When you see thieves, you befriend them;
    with adulterers you throw in your lot. . . .

"Understand this, you who forget God,
    lest I attack you with no one to rescue.
Those who offer praise as a sacrifice honor me;
    to the obedient I will show the salvation of God."
        (Ps 50:7-11, 14-18, 22-23)

In the view of the Old Testament a sacrifice of praise was the prayer and sacrifice offered by a person whose daily living was consistent with the attitudes toward God and others expressed by such a sacrifice. In a sacrifice of praise the rite of sacrifice one physically performed and the words of sacrifice one spoke expressed the real self-giving of one's heart. At times this language of sacrifice even became completely metaphorical and spiritualized, as a way of speaking about a person's sincere praise, repentance, and humility before God (see, for example, Ps 51:19).[23]

Our offering to God, the Roman Canon insists, can never be a charade, as if we might convince God of our sincerity by going through the motions. It's not magic, as though it has value simply

---

23. Xavier Leon-Dufour, SJ, *Sharing the Eucharistic Bread: The Witness of the New Testament*, tr. Matthew J. O'Connell (New York: Paulist Press, 1987), 40–44.

because we say the right words. Our repeated prayer that God accept our offering should cause us to ask ourselves if we're mocking the offering by the lives we live, and push us to make our prayer more authentic by living more consistently.[24]

Giving Only What We've Been Given

One more venerable phrase from the Roman Canon, related to sacrifice, is worth a moment's reflection. The *Unde et memores*, the Canon's memorial, proclaims that what we offer to God ("this pure victim, this holy victim, this spotless victim, the holy Bread of eternal life and the Chalice of everlasting salvation") is "from the gifts that you [Lord] have given us."

Here the Canon echoes the prayer of King David after offering his own riches as well as the personal treasures collected from the Israelites for use in the temple of the Lord. In the presence of the assembly of Israel, David prayed: "But who am I, and who are my people, that we should have the means to contribute so freely? For everything is from you, and we only give you what we have received from you" (1 Chr 29:14).

Our sacrifice is only a return of the gifts God has first given us. We are no better off than a child who can only buy his parents a Christmas present from the money they have given him as allowance. I'd suggest that this affirmation should provoke in us humility, but also gratitude, for so great is God's generosity toward us that what we have to offer is of infinite value.

"God gives that we may give." Joseph Ratzinger calls this "the essence of the Eucharistic Sacrifice."[25] In fact, he points beautifully to the sacrifice of Abraham, who was given a ram by God to sacrifice in the place of his son Isaac: "this lamb in the brambles that God gives him, so that he may offer it, is the first herald of that Lamb, Jesus Christ, who carries the crown of thorns of our

---

24. Cf. ibid., 74.

25. Joseph Cardinal Ratzinger, *God Is Near Us: The Eucharist, the Heart of Life*, tr. Henry Taylor (San Francisco: Ignatius Press, 2003), 47.

guilt, who has come into the thorn bush of world history in order to give us something that we may give."[26]

We see this same idea in some earlier anaphoras, such as the Liturgy of St. John Chrysostom and the Byzantine Liturgy of St. Basil, both of which speak of the assembly "offering you your own from your own."[27] In the anaphoras of today's Roman Missal we find it outside the Roman Canon in Eucharistic Prayer IV, in which the second epiclesis asks the Lord to "Look . . . upon the Sacrifice which you yourself have provided for your Church." And in the memorial of Eucharistic Prayer for Masses of Reconciliation II we pray: "We celebrate the memory of this death and resurrection and bring you the gift you have given us, the sacrifice of reconciliation."

The Eucharist confirms our conviction: all is grace.

---

26. Ibid., 46. Mention of the sacrifice of Abraham follows immediately in the Canon, in the *Supra que*, along with those of Abel and Melchizedek. Note, too, that for St. Thomas Aquinas our sacrifice stands in the same relationship as theirs, except that theirs prefigured Christ's while ours commemorates it (Mazza, *The Eucharistic Prayers*, 80 n. 127).

27. R. C. D. Jasper and G. J. Cuming, eds., *Prayers of the Eucharist: Early and Reformed*, 3d ed. (Collegeville, MN: Liturgical Press, 1990), 133, 119.

Eucharistic Prayer II:
"To Break the Bonds of Death"

It probably makes the liturgical scholars grind their teeth with frustration, but Eucharistic Prayer II—which is fascinating and even historic for several important reasons—is known by most Mass-going Catholics for one thing: it's the short one! Hearing the opening words to this anaphora has brought a quiet sigh of relief from more than a few impatient Massgoers in recent decades. (Of course, having read this book, you will never find yourself in that category again!) Indeed, when it was first introduced in 1969 this prayer was praised by some scholars for its conciseness and simplicity, and criticized by others as a scandal because what is supposed to be the culmination of all the church's worship of God is reduced to a few terse lines.

But it would be a shame if all we knew about this prayer is that it helps us get home on time to catch the opening kickoff of Sunday's football game. Let's take a look.

Deep Roots, Many Questions

Eucharistic Prayer II has an interesting background, with a history that goes far back, certainly prior to our earliest records of the Roman Canon. But we don't know as much about its history as we used to think.

When Pope Paul VI gave permission to the Consilium in 1967 to compose some new eucharistic prayers that might be used in the Roman rite, the ancient anaphora of the *Apostolic Tradition* (which we looked at in chapter 3) seemed to be one obvious source from which to work.[1] At the time this ancient document was generally believed to have been composed by Hippolytus in Rome around 215. Today further research has raised significant doubts about its title, author, and date of composition. Though some scholars still maintain that Hippolytus wrote it, others argue that it is not the work of a single author at all, but a collection of materials written at different times (as early as the mid-second century and as late as the mid-fourth) and places (Syria? Rome?).[2] Another uncertainty is whether the liturgy it describes represents the way the Eucharist was conducted in Rome, Syria, or elsewhere—or maybe just the liturgy as its author thought it *should have been* celebrated.

The very title is puzzling too. It's never mentioned on the existing copies of the document itself. Rather, it comes from a headless statue discovered in Rome in 1551, thought to be of Hippolytus of Rome. (Even this statue is an enigma. Archaeological studies have concluded that it was originally a female figure but was restored in the sixteenth century, using parts from other statues, to be a male bishop!)[3] The Greek inscription on the statue's base lists the subject's works, including one called *Apostolic Tradition*. Based on the similarity of the document in question to two other documents already known to be written by Hippolytus of Rome, it was thought that this was in fact the work listed on the statue. But some scholars disagree, and the question is far from settled.[4]

If the *Apostolic Tradition* was written by Hippolytus of Rome, that adds to its interest, because he has an intriguing story of his own. Hippolytus was a priest in Rome who had serious disagreements with Rome's bishop, Callistus.

1. Annibale Bugnini, *The Reform of the Liturgy 1948–1975*, tr. Matthew J. O'Connell (Collegeville, MN: Liturgical Press, 1990), 450 n. 4.

2. Paul F. Bradshaw and others, *The Apostolic Tradition: A Commentary*, Hermeneia (Minneapolis: Fortress Press, 2002), 14.

3. Ibid., 4.

4. Ibid., 2–4; Paul F. Bradshaw, *The Search for the Origins of Christian Worship: Sources and Methods for the Study of Early Liturgy* (New York: Oxford University Press, 1992), 90–91.

Much of their conflict regarded what was to be done about the *lapsi*, Christians who had given in, during times of the church's persecution, to pressures to deny their faith when they were threatened with imprisonment, torture, or death. Callistus believed in dealing mercifully with them; Hippolytus thought he was being weak and unfaithful to his role of teacher and defender of the faith. So intense did the conflict become that Hippolytus's supporters elected him an antipope.

But God has a sense of humor, and the Romans had no interest in splitting hairs about who was right in such arguments. Callistus passed away, and Hippolytus continued his opposition to his successor, Pontian. When Hippolytus was arrested for his Christian faith and forced into exile he found himself accompanied by Pontian, who had suffered the same fate. It was during this time that Hippolytus reconciled himself with Pontian and with the church. They were both martyred, and today they share a common feast day, August 13.[5] The irony of their shared feast is beautiful: the pope and the antipope who opposed him, reconciled during the persecution they underwent together and then martyred for the faith in Christ that they shared.

Whether or not St. Hippolytus wrote it, the *Apostolic Tradition* offers us a remarkable look at an early celebration of the Eucharist. It contains what is almost certainly the earliest example we have of an actual eucharistic prayer. Take another look at the anaphora of the *Apostolic Tradition* presented in chapter 3. (Remember, though, that this was an age when those who presided at the Eucharist usually had the freedom to extemporize the anaphora they prayed.)

It's a beautiful prayer, and we needn't be scholars to pick out many of the typical structural parts of the eucharistic prayer that we looked at in Part Two of this book. After an introductory dialogue (to which the one used in the Roman rite today is almost identical), it opens with a preface that gives thanks to God for the gift of his Son Jesus Christ. This leads into a remarkable description

5. R. C. D. Jasper and G. J. Cuming, *Prayers of the Eucharist: Early and Reformed*, 3d ed. (Collegeville, MN: Liturgical Press, 1990), 36.

of Christ's Paschal Mystery, his suffering, dying, and rising again for our salvation. This is followed by a memorial and offering, a robust epiclesis, a unique doxology, and an Amen.

Strong Words

It's hard to miss the dramatic imagery the prayer uses to speak of Jesus' saving work as a triumph over the power of sin and Satan, accomplished "in order to destroy death and to break the chains of the devil, to tread down hell beneath his feet, to bring out the righteous into light, to set the term and to manifest the resurrection."[6] But look again, and you'll probably see even more than you did with a first reading.

Notice the very extended opening sentence following the initial dialogue, which comprises a long preface and moves right into the institution narrative. This sentence is difficult to offer readably in English, and most translations of the anaphora break it up into many independent sentences. But to do so is to lose the opportunity for some important insights into the prayer.

This passage is made up of a series of dependent clauses, all of which refer to "your beloved Child Jesus Christ." What follows describes the work of Jesus as the one "whom you have sent . . . who is your inseparable Word . . . who, having been conceived, became incarnate . . . who fulfilling your will and acquiring for you a holy people, stretched out his hands . . . who . . . in order to destroy death and to break the chains of the devil . . ." and so on. What's more interesting is that the institution narrative is actually the last element of this series of clauses: ". . . who . . . taking bread, gave thanks to you and said, Take, eat. . . ."

Especially worth noticing here is that the institution narrative represents an integral part of this wonderful reflection on who Christ is and what he has done for us. The Last Supper—and also the eucharistic celebration in which we recite this narra-

---

6. Peter G. Cobb, "The *Apostolic Tradition* of Hippolytus," in Cheslyn Jones and others, eds., *The Study of Liturgy*, rev. ed. (London: SPCK, 1992), 214.

tive—is presented brilliantly as the culminating element of the divine assault on death and the devil!

If asked how Jesus destroyed death, conquered Satan, and the like, most people with even a basic familiarity with Christian theology would answer, through his death and resurrection. True as that is, it's not the idea we find in this anaphora. Follow its complex sentence structure, and you find a different and startling answer: "in order to destroy death and to break the chains of the devil, to tread down hell beneath his feet, to bring out the righteous into light, to set the term and to manifest the resurrection, [Jesus] *taking bread, gave thanks to you and said, Take, eat. . . .*"

To kill death and conquer Satan, it says, *Jesus celebrated the supper*. That is, he instituted the sacrament by which his redemption is made accessible to us!

Mazza coins a perfectly apt term when he writes that this prayer, in a unique way, *paschalizes* the Eucharist. It suggests that Christ's Paschal Mystery should not be described as his "suffering, death, and resurrection," but rather his "last supper, suffering, death, and resurrection." It draws out for the worshiping church the intrinsic and essential connection between the Paschal Mystery of Jesus Christ and the Eucharist that church gathers to celebrate.[7]

Reaching Back

The Consilium that prepared the eucharistic prayers for the 1969 reform of the liturgy decided it could not attempt simply to introduce the prayer of the *Apostolic Tradition* in its ancient form into the contemporary liturgy. For one thing, some of the ancient language was less than clear to modern ears. (Jesus is an "angel"? What does it mean when it says that Jesus "fix[ed] a term"?) For another, they decided that all the new eucharistic prayers would have the same basic structure, and some parts, like the Sanctus and the words of institution, would be completely identical in all

---

7. Enrico Mazza, *The Eucharistic Prayers of the Roman Rite* (New York: Pueblo, 1986), 96.

of them. Since Hippolytus's prayer did not even have a Sanctus, memorial acclamation, or consecratory epiclesis, that meant making some significant additions and revisions to get it ready for a new life in the modern-day liturgy.

Taking a closer look, we can see exactly why Eucharistic Prayer II ends up being such a short one. Following the opening dialogue (which is identical in all the new prayers), we find the preface. Let's skip that temporarily, because we're going to dwell on it in a moment.

After the preface is the Sanctus (which, as we said, is the same in all the new eucharistic prayers, but was not in the original prayer from the *Apostolic Tradition*). Following the Sanctus, Eucharistic Prayer II continues momentarily on the theme of God's holiness ("You are indeed Holy, O Lord, the fount of all holiness") and then moves immediately into the first epiclesis. It is brief but beautiful, asking God to send the Spirit upon the gifts "like the dewfall."

The prayer then moves immediately into the institution narrative, which is followed by the memorial acclamation (both of which are also identical in all four eucharistic prayers). They are followed by the memorial and offering (combined into one sentence), the epiclesis over the people (one sentence), and intercessions for the church, for her leaders and clergy, and for the dead. The doxology and amen (both the same in all four eucharistic prayers) conclude it. For better or worse, then, this prayer truly moves in rapid succession through each of these elements. Each part is accomplished as concisely as possible, with very little time or words spent dwelling upon or drawing out the ideas they express.

A Hymn of Thanksgiving

Given all that, the section to which our attention is naturally drawn, then, is the preface. This section alone is allowed space for its ideas to develop and be drawn out, if only for a few lines. What results is an extraordinary piece of liturgical prayer, confessing the essentials of the church's Gospel in two developed sentences that are structured in such a way that they yield more and more richness with each hearing.

Remember, the preface is about thanksgiving. The opening dialogue has concluded with the celebrant calling upon the congregation to join him: "Let us give thanks to the Lord." With their agreement ("It is right and just"), he enters into a hymn of thanksgiving to God, our "Father most holy, through your beloved Son, Jesus Christ." This sentence continues, describing Jesus as "your Word through whom you made all things, whom you sent as our Savior and Redeemer," and it's that description I'd like to consider.

The first phrase is a clear reference to the christological hymn of Colossians 1, "one of the most important theological statements about the person of Christ in the New Testament."[8] Perhaps borrowed by Paul from the early Christian liturgy,[9] it speaks of Christ's involvement in the work of the creation of the universe:

> He is the image of the invisible God,
> the firstborn of all creation.
> For in him were created all things in heaven and on earth,
> the visible and the invisible,
> whether thrones or dominions or principalities or
> powers;
> all things were created through him and for him.
> He is before all things,
> and in him all things hold together. (Col 1:15-17)

Our thanksgiving to God is for the work of creation, accomplished through Christ at the beginning of time.

The second phrase draws on rich scriptural teaching about Jesus as the savior and redeemer of the world. It calls to mind the angel's announcement to the shepherds that "a savior has been born for you" (Luke 2:11), the recognition of Jesus as "savior of the world" by the woman at the well (John 4:42), and the

---

8. Ivan Havener, OSB, "Colossians," in Dianne Bergant, CSA, and Robert J. Karris, OFM, eds., *The Collegeville Bible Commentary* (Collegeville, MN: Liturgical Press, 1989), 1182.

9. Cf. Joseph A. Grassi, "The Letter to the Colossians," in Raymond E. Brown, SS, Joseph A. Fitzmyer, SJ, and Roland E. Murphy, OCarm., eds., *The Jerome Biblical Commentary* (Englewood Cliffs, NJ: Prentice-Hall, 1968), 336.

nascent church's confession of him in the same terms (for example, in Acts 12:23; 1 Tim 4:10; Titus 1:4). Here the church joins the angels, the woman, Peter, and Paul in making the same proclamation in its liturgy, and at the same time giving thanks for the gift of redemption received. So we are thanking God in our preface for the two most fundamental things for which we will always have to give thanks, the two great works of God: creation and redemption.

Notice that the prayer relates both these divine works *to* Christ *as he relates to* the Father. We thank the Father for creation, which he worked through his Son, his Word; we thank the Father for redemption, for which he sent his Son, the Savior and Redeemer. And we thank him for these things, which he accomplished in Christ, through Christ himself.

Destroying Death

The next set of lines in this preface is also worth some reflection. Recalling the *Apostolic Tradition*'s distinctive paschalization of the Eucharist, we can say that Eucharistic Prayer II's greatest shortcoming may be that it has fundamentally *de*-paschalized the original prayer.[10] Much of the powerful imagery and certainly the distinctive sentence structure has been removed. A few lines of Eucharistic Prayer II's preface are really all that remain of it— which is all the more reason to allow them to hit us with their full force: "Fulfilling your will and gaining for you a holy people, he stretched out his hands as he endured his Passion, *so as to break the bonds of death and manifest the resurrection.*"

Here we should have it clear in our minds that the death of which the prayer speaks, the death whose bonds Christ broke, is ours—yours and mine. It is the death of each member of our families, of each person with whom we work and rest and dine and worship. Christ "killed death" for all of us.

The resurrection he manifested is not only his own but ours as well. It was not Christ who "needed" resurrection. After all,

---

10. Cf. Mazza, *The Eucharistic Prayers*, 105–8.

long before he died and rose, Christ announced, "I am the resurrection and the life." Christ rose from the dead for us, in order to win for us new and glorified life. We can see this expressed beautifully in eastern icons of the resurrection, which depict Jesus standing over the shattered gates of hell while he pulls Adam and Eve (who represent us) from their own coffins.

These ideas would be "Good News" in any context. But here they come in the church's liturgy, in which "the work of our redemption is accomplished,"[11] and in the church's eucharistic prayer, in which the Eucharist becomes the memorial of our redemption—all of which means that even as this salvation is proclaimed it becomes effective in us. The Eucharist imparts to us, makes present in us, Christ's redemptive work. As the priest before us prays that Christ broke the bonds of death, the bonds of death break in us. As he speaks of Christ manifesting his resurrection, his glorified life is manifested in us.

In fact, recall the unique way in which the anaphora of the *Apostolic Tradition* connected Christ's triumphant paschal mystery with the institution narrative by making them each elements of a series of dependent clauses, all of which referred to Christ himself, the Savior and Redeemer. Unfortunately, with the addition of the Sanctus and first epiclesis to the source prayer this direct structural connection is no longer present in Eucharistic Prayer II. No longer is breaking the bonds of death presented as the reason for the supper. They are two distinct and separate facts in two different parts of the prayer.

Still, with its deep roots in liturgical history, Eucharistic Prayer II stands as a succinct and effective proclamation in our own day of the Good News of Jesus.

---

11. From the Prayer over the Gifts, Holy Thursday evening liturgy. Cf. Kevin W. Irwin, *Context and Text: Method in Liturgical Theology* (Collegeville, MN: Liturgical Press, 1994), 186 n. 45.

Eucharistic Prayer III:
"To Gather a People"

One thing I hope is becoming clear is that each of these eucharistic prayers is fascinating in its own way, for its own reasons. Eucharistic Prayer III is no exception.

We have seen that Eucharistic Prayer I has its roots in the fourth century, and that Eucharistic Prayer II was strongly influenced by an anaphora from the third century. We will see in the next chapter that Eucharistic Prayer IV has its own early and interesting influences.

With Eucharistic Prayer III we don't have direct and deep historical roots to point to. Of the four, it's the closest we come in the 1969 liturgical reform to a truly contemporary eucharistic prayer. We know that the Italian theologian Cipriano Vagaggini was particularly influential in its composition.[1] Pope Paul VI took a particular interest in this prayer, so much so that one scholar maintains: "When historians come to give it a name they will have no choice but to call it the 'Canon of Paul VI.' "[2]

Like the Roman Canon, Eucharistic Prayer III includes a variable preface. This is a distinctive feature of the Roman rite, but both of the other two primary eucharistic prayers come with their

1. Enrico Mazza, *The Eucharistic Prayers of the Roman Rite*, tr. Matthew J. O'Connell (New York: Pueblo, 1986), 125. Mazza also cites (p. 318 n. 10), Annibale Bugnini's clear attestation to this (*The Reform of the Liturgy 1948–1975*, tr. Matthew J. O'Connell [Collegeville, MN: Liturgical Press, 1990]).

2. Mazza, *The Eucharistic Prayers*, 125 (citing, and agreeing with, Theodor Schnitzler, *I tre nuovi canoni ed i nuovi prefazi nella predicazione e meditazione* [Rome: Edizioni Paoline, 1970], 62).

own prefaces included—Eucharistic Prayer II has an optional one, though others may be substituted; Eucharistic Prayer IV has its own, which may never be replaced. This makes Eucharistic Prayer III "the prayer of festive days"[3]—an appropriate choice in order to make use of the special prefaces provided for use on particular Sundays and feast days of the year.

Three themes are strong in the prayer: the holiness of God, sacrifice, and the church. Of these, the ecclesiological theme is clearly dominant. Let's take a look.

Sharing in the Holiness of God

Following whichever preface is chosen, Eucharistic Prayer III, like the other eucharistic prayers, proclaims the holiness of God in the Sanctus. In each of those others the presider makes reference to God's holiness at least briefly, as a means of transition from the Sanctus to the rest of the prayer (hence the name of this segment of the prayer, the post-Sanctus). But a careful listener can discern that in Eucharistic Prayer III the theme of holiness is picked up after the Sanctus and carried through just about the entire prayer. Notice first the construction of the post-Sanctus. The opening lines of its English text are below on the left, while my simplification (without regard for beauty) on the right is intended to help make its structure clear, like looking at the framework of a car after its flashy body has been removed.

You are indeed Holy, O Lord,	You are holy, Lord
and all you have created	and all creation
rightly gives you praise,	praises you,
for through your Son our Lord Jesus Christ,	because (through Jesus
by the power and working of the Holy Spirit,	and the Spirit)
you give life to all things and make them holy . . .	you give life and holiness to it all.

---

3. Mazza, *The Eucharistic Prayers*, 123.

Having acclaimed the holiness of God in the Sanctus, we proclaim that all creation offers praise not only because God is holy, but also because God has shared his holiness with all things!

Following upon this, the next section, the epiclesis, begins with *therefore*. This not only connects the epiclesis with the post-Sanctus; it also suggests that what we do in the epiclesis comes *as a result of* the reality we're proclaiming in the post-Sanctus: "Therefore, O Lord, we humbly implore you: by the same Spirit graciously make holy these gifts we have brought to you for consecration."

Because God is holy and *because* God has shared his holiness with all creatures, we *therefore* ask him to make holy the gifts we bring. The consecration—the making holy—of the bread and wine is presented *in the context of* the holiness of God, which God has already shared with all creation. This "flow of holiness" expressed in the prayer can be illustrated this way:

Holiness of God	→	Holiness of creation	→	Holiness of the consecrated gifts

But if we continue to follow along, the grammatical structure hints at still more. Following the epiclesis, the institution narrative begins, and it opens with the conjunction *for*, another grammatical connection to what has come before. "For on the night he was betrayed, . . ." *Because of* what Jesus did and said on the night he was betrayed, we who are assembled here implore God to make holy the gifts we offer now.

Later, in the anamnesis, we return again to the idea of holiness: what we offer to God is "this holy and living sacrifice." Earlier we asked him to make our offering holy. Now we express our trust in his response: this sacrifice is holy.

Note the two adjectives, which echo perfectly the two gifts we said God gives to all things back in the post-Sanctus: life and holiness. This parallel certainly strengthens the assertion that the holiness of the gifts we consecrate is seen in this prayer within the context of the holiness of all things, which share in God's own holiness.

This is not at all to minimize the uniqueness of the eucharistic consecration. Throughout the Old Testament, for example, we see that God, who shares his holiness with all creation, shares it in a particular way with certain places, people, and times. These were, in fact, usually associated with worship (temple, priest, offerings, Sabbath, etc).[4] It was through their worship, involving these sacred realities, that the whole Israelite people shared in God's holiness. In the new covenant, through the Eucharist, God's creation and his people share in that holiness in a particular way.

A Pure Sacrifice

The fathers of the church saw the Eucharist as a fulfillment of the words of the prophet Malachi: "From the rising of the sun to its setting my name is great among the nations, and in every place incense is offered to my name, and a pure offering; for my name is great among the nations, says the Lord of hosts."[5] It seems that the twentieth-century reformers of Catholic liturgy were just as keen to make this connection, putting on the presider's lips in the post-Sanctus the conviction that "you never cease to gather a people to yourself, so that from the rising of the sun to its setting a pure sacrifice may be offered to your name."

But this is only the beginning of the presence of the idea of sacrifice in Eucharistic Prayer III. The German scholar Herman Wegman worded it strongly when he called Eucharistic Prayer III "a 'sacrificial Canon,' for the idea of sacrifice and the word itself recur constantly in its paragraphs and lines; they are present in every individual part and give it its precise and essential meaning."[6] In fact, if it has any model at all in the anaphoral tradition, it seems to be the Roman Canon itself, which, as we noted in chapter 20, is so strongly sacrificial in theme.[7]

---

4. Cf. Xavier Léon-Dufour, ed., *Dictionary of Biblical Theology*, 2d ed. (Gaithersburg, MD: Word Among Us; Boston: Pauline Books and Media, 1988), 237.

5. Mazza, *The Eucharistic Prayers*, 127.

6. Cited in ibid., 124–25.

7. Mazza asserts this, agreeing (ibid., 124) with Wegman (*Christian Worship in East and West: A Study Guide to Liturgical History*, tr. Gordon W. Lathrop

In addition to the lines of the post-Sanctus just noted,[8] consider:

☐ We refer in the anamnesis to "this holy and living sacrifice."

☐ We then ask God to "look . . . upon the oblation of your Church,"

☐ and, looking upon it, to "recogniz[e] the sacrificial Victim by whose death you willed to reconcile us to yourself."[9]

☐ Continuing the sacrificial theme, we ask God to "make of us an eternal offering."

☐ In the intercessions we refer to this celebration of the Eucharist as "this Sacrifice of our reconciliation."[10]

☐ And, of course, the sacrificial words and imagery of the institution narrative are an integral part of this eucharistic prayer as well.

It is interesting that some theologians and preachers, following the Second Vatican Council, seemed almost to abandon the idea of the sacrificial nature of the Eucharist, yet this most contemporary of the three new eucharistic prayers, produced immediately following the council and so clearly rooted in its teaching, emphasizes the Eucharist's sacrificial nature resoundingly. If we take this prayer as our *lex orandi*, we know that the Eucharist we celebrate is sacrificial; that it is our sacrifice; that what we offer in sacrifice is both Christ and ourselves (the idea of offering ourselves along with Christ is probably clearer in this

---

[Collegeville, MN: Liturgical Press, 1990]). As I will point out below, the theme of the church is very strong in Eucharistic Prayer III; we've already noted that the same can be said about the Roman Canon.

8. Like this line from Eucharistic Prayer III, the Roman Canon is also preoccupied with the purity of the sacrifice that is offered. We see this in both the *Te igitur* and the *Unde et memores*.

9. "Victim," however, may not be the best word to use in translating the Latin *hostia*, or the one intended by the composers of the prayer. See Mazza, *The Eucharistic Prayers*, 136–37. We see reference to the Victim being offered in Eucharistic Prayer I as well, in the *Unde et memores* (where a problem with the use of "Victim" is even more significant) and the *Supra que*.

10. An idea expressed in Eucharistic Prayer I's *Memento Domini* in its statement that the sacrifice is offered "for the redemption of [the offerers'] souls."

prayer than in any of the others); and that the sacrifice we offer reconciles us to God.

The Church: At the Heart of the Gospel

A still stronger theme in this eucharistic prayer is that of the church. This should probably come as no surprise. As we've said above, this prayer represents the most contemporary expression of eucharistic praying among the three new prayers of the 1969 Missal. It was composed following several decades of renewal, in both Catholic theology and Catholic doctrine, in understanding the nature of the church.[11] This deepened understanding, profoundly scriptural in nature, is reflected in the prayer. And, of course, it was also composed immediately following the ecumenical council that produced the Dogmatic Constitution on the Church (*Lumen Gentium*).

But the nature of the church is more than just the theological enthusiasm of that particular moment. It is in fact a central theme—it could even be called *the* central theme—of the entire Gospel. It is what the Christian faith, and in particular the Christian Eucharist, is all about.

An exaggeration? Not at all. It's there from beginning to end. Genesis tells of humanity being created in the image of God, a God who would later reveal himself as a communion of divine Persons. Sin is depicted there from the start as profoundly divisive (Adam and Eve alienated from one another, one of their sons killing the other, and, of course, Babel). God's intervention, his remedy to the situation brought about by sin, was to call together a people, whose very self-identity was *qahal*, "assembly" (see, for example, Deut 23:2 and Judg 20:2), expressed most clearly in the gathering at Sinai, but also later reinstituted, following the exile (a dispersion), by Ezra.

In the Christian reading of this Israelite history, this gathering was a foreshadowing and preparation for what would come later,

---

11. The work of Henri de Lubac and Yves Congar stands out in the theology of the period. Doctrinally, Pius XII's 1947 encyclical *Mystici Corporis* was a landmark that led the way to *Lumen Gentium*.

the penultimate gathering-in of God's people by Jesus, the good shepherd, who came "to gather into one the dispersed children of God" (John 11:52). And how does he gather? Primarily, in his Paschal Mystery: "When I am lifted up from the earth, I will draw everyone to myself" (John 12:32-33).[12] The twentieth-century scholar Joachim Jeremias put it plainly: "We must reduce the whole question quite sharply to a single point: the sole meaning of the entire activity of Jesus is the gathering of the eschatological people of God."[13] Eschatological, because the final and full gathering-in is still to come. It will take place in the New Jerusalem, among "countless angels in festal gathering, and the assembly of the firstborn enrolled in heaven" (Heb 12:22).

Eucharistic Prayer III calls all of this to mind from the post-Sanctus, when we pray to the Father: "you never cease to gather a people to yourself."[14] We hear it in the intercessions, when we pray for the church by calling it "the entire people you have gained for your own," and a moment later when the assembly gathered for Mass is called "this family, whom you have summoned before you." And we hear it one more time, with particularly strong echoes of the two passages from John cited above, when we ask the Father to "gather to yourself all your children scattered throughout the earth."[15] This ecclesiological theme becomes the prism through which many other ideas and themes of Eucharistic Prayer III—including the Trinity, liturgy, sacrifice, and the saints—can be read.

The post-Sanctus, for example, is notably trinitarian. But the references to the three Persons of the Trinity seem to lead up to

12. The entire Gospel of John is rich in the theme of Jesus as gatherer. Passages like the two just cited, along with others such as John 10:1-16; 11:45-54; 17:1-20, just begin to scratch the surface of this.

13. Cited in Joseph Cardinal Ratzinger, *Called to Communion: Understanding the Church Today*, tr. Adrian Walker (San Francisco: Ignatius Press, 1996), 22.

14. For example, Mazza comments: "We can hear in the background an echo of the Exodus and themes of Passover" (*The Eucharistic Prayers*, 127).

15. The newer ICEL translation, while more faithful to the Latin typical edition, also more effectively points to the Scripture passage in which it is rooted. The previous English translation asked God to "unite all your children wherever they may be."

and culminate in the reference to the fundamental work of the Trinity in salvation history: the gathering of God's people. The passage seems almost intentionally to call to mind *Lumen Gentium*, which quotes St. Cyprian when it teaches that "the universal Church is seen to be 'a people brought into unity from the unity of the Father, the Son, and the Holy Spirit.'"[16] The ecclesiology also becomes liturgical when the prayer continues, noting that God gathers this people "so that from the rising of the sun to its setting a pure sacrifice may be offered to your name." The church is understood as an assembly gathered for the purpose of sacrificial praise, gathered for liturgy.[17]

The same ecclesiological reading is wrapped into the theology of the eucharistic sacrifice when the Eucharist is called "the oblation of your Church." And, in fact, Eucharistic Prayer III suggests that what is offered in this oblation is not only the elements of bread and wine, and not only Christ, but also itself, the gathered assembly: "make of us an eternal offering."

The intercessions include prayer for the church: "confirm in faith and charity your pilgrim Church on earth."[18] Indeed, a bit earlier, in the commemoration of the saints, Eucharistic Prayer III becomes the only one of the four primary eucharistic prayers to explicitly include a place for the presider to mention the saint of the day or the local patron saint. Given the importance of the role of the Communion of Saints in ecclesiology, this is significant. (In fact, given this unique element of Eucharistic Prayer III, its similarities with Eucharistic Prayer I, and its particularly contemporary nature, it would have been very interesting to see in this prayer an extended list of saints, along the lines of those found in Eucharistic Prayer I but representing saints from various places and times in the long history of the church.)

16. LG 4.
17. Mazza, *The Eucharistic Prayers*, 127.
18. Mazza notes the connection here with Eph 4:15-16.

Eucharistic Prayer IV: "To the Praise of Your Glory"

Eucharistic Prayer IV dropped, in 1969, like a comet from a different solar system into the Roman liturgical tradition. To speak of it as a unique feature in the history of the Roman rite is an understatement—this to the delight of some and the chagrin of others. Despite this, its infrequency of use by presiders over the last four decades has left it still unfamiliar to many, even most, practicing Catholics. (Reasons offered for this lack of use generally tend to touch on two issues: its length, and its use of exclusive language, references to humanity as "man" and with the masculine pronouns.)

Despite its novelty in the West, taking a look into some other corners of Christendom's liturgical universe reveals some good company. In style and structure Eucharistic Prayer IV is clearly influenced by the Eastern tradition. Recalling the image from chapter 3 of the fourth- and fifth-century Eastern anaphoras being like a thick-growing garden, heavy in fruits and rich in blossoms, we might say that with the introduction of Eucharistic Prayer IV it is as though a large chunk of such a garden were transplanted— fruits, shoots, and flowers—into the more stately fields of the Roman rite.

The anaphoras that seem most clearly to have served as direct sources for Eucharistic Prayer IV are those of the *Apostolic Constitutions*,[1] the Byzantine Liturgy of St. Basil[2] (both of which come

---

1. R. C. D. Jasper and G. J. Cuming, *Prayers of the Eucharist: Early and Reformed*, 3d ed. (Collegeville: Liturgical Press, 1990), 100–13.
2. Ibid., 114–23.

from fourth-century Antioch), and the Liturgy of St. James[3] (used in Palestine in the early Middle Ages). The second of these remains in occasional use today in the ancient Eastern Christian church.

A Summary of Salvation History

One of the most important things to be said about Eucharistic Prayer IV is already stated in its very first rubric as it is printed in the Roman Missal. The rubric notes that no other preface may be substituted for the one that is included with the text of the anaphora, and it adds an explanatory clause in the same sentence: "because of the structure of the Prayer itself, which presents a summary of salvation history."

In Roman tradition the most important moments and stages of God's revelation and humanity's redemption are celebrated in its eucharistic prayer gradually throughout the year, primarily through the variable prefaces that are provided for different seasons and feasts. But with Eucharistic Prayer IV all of salvation history is presented through the course of the text of one anaphora. Therefore, to put a different preface in place of the prayer's own would be to sunder the structure of the prayer and distort its content.

All anaphoras are in some way creedal—they're all a profession of the Christian faith they celebrate.[4] But Eucharistic Prayer IV is especially creedal; a rich and beautiful theological account of the nature of God and his redemptive work in human history is carried on through the text. Largely for this reason Mazza calls it "the most theological of all the Eucharistic prayers."[5]

The preface opens by bearing witness, with thanks and praise, to Christian faith in *who God is*. The prayer proclaims him to be

3. Ibid., 88–99.

4. Cf. Enrico Mazza, *The Eucharistic Prayers of the Roman Rite*, tr. Matthew J. O'Connell (New York: Pueblo, 1986), 158–60; Robert J. Ledogar, "The Eucharistic Prayer and the Gifts Over Which It Is Spoken," in R. Kevin Seasoltz, OSB, ed., *Living Bread, Saving Cup: Readings on the Eucharist* (Collegeville, MN: Liturgical Press, 1987), 63.

5. Mazza, *The Eucharistic Prayers*, 157.

the "one God living and true, existing before all ages and abiding for all eternity, dwelling in unapproachable light." It then moves from an account of the nature of God to *the work of God in creation*. He is "the source of life" who "made all that is" in order to bless his creatures and "bring joy to many of them by the glory of your light."

Following the Sanctus, the prayer provides further account of Christian faith in God and his work, here highlighting *God's trinitarian nature* and work of *redemption*. The three stanzas there—unusually long for the portion between the Sanctus and the first epiclesis—deal with the redemptive work in history of the Father, the Son, and the Holy Spirit, respectively.

The Father is presented as the creator of all, and particularly of humanity, made in his own image. It notes that God "entrusted the whole world" to humanity's care, giving humanity "dominion over all creatures," then calls to mind the "disobedience" by which we "lost [God's] friendship." Following these references to the opening chapters of Genesis, the central narrative of the Old Testament is summarized by saying that "time and again you offered them covenants and through the prophets taught them to look forward to salvation." Reference to the covenants and the prophets without mention of the Law may represent a lacuna here.

The beginning of the next stanza blends the work of the Father into the mission of the Son, with the elision of two paraphrases, from John 3:16 and Galatians 4:4, proclaiming that God "so loved the world" that "in the fullness of time" he sent his Son "to be our Savior." With references to the Incarnation and Christ's proclamation of the Good News of freedom and joy, this section culminates with the paschal mystery of Christ's death and resurrection, by which he "destroyed death and restored life."

As the second stanza of the section opened by blending the work of the Father and the Son, the third opens by blending the work of the Son and the Holy Spirit. Making effective the Son's mission is presented as the end of the work of the Spirit, who is sent from the Father "that we might live no longer for ourselves but for him who died and rose again for us." It is the Spirit who "bring[s] to perfection [Christ's] work in the world."

And don't miss the final trinitarian flourish that closes this section with the proclamation that the Spirit works "so that . . . he [the Son] might sanctify [in the Spirit] creation [the Father's work] to the full." In choosing to present salvation history within this Trinitarian structure this post-Sanctus section achieves what the preface also does—it celebrates God in his own eternal nature as well as in his work in history.

Another reference to covenant, this one the "eternal covenant" left to us by Christ, appears in the first epiclesis, and then more language that is distinctly Johannine introduces the institution narrative. Consistent with the content and style of this prayer, the memorial is especially robust; besides the suffering, death, and resurrection of Christ, it also mentions his "descent to the realm of the dead" (a mystery of Christ that is mentioned in no other present eucharistic prayer of the Roman rite) and "his coming in glory," which we await (mentioned in few of them).

For good reason, then, Eucharistic Prayer IV has been called "a long but beautiful anamnesis of the entire history of salvation."[6] That most Catholics rarely hear it proclaimed is unfortunate. Familiarity with its contents would provide the Catholic people— who are often notoriously ignorant of their own Scriptures—with an extraordinary reference with which to understand the Christian story in general and also to contextualize the Scripture readings they hear proclaimed in the Mass's Liturgy of the Word.[7]

A Prayer of Joy in God

Certainly this prayer's presentation of the entirety of salvation history is a distinctive feature. But what we're talking about here is more than a poetic theology lesson. This is not just a liturgical listing of God's redemptive works. Rather, the account

6. Salvatore Marsili and others, eds., *Eucaristia: teologia e storia della celebrazione* (Casale Monferrato: Marietti, 1983), 254 (my translation).

7. Cf. Consilium for the Implementation of the Constitution on the Liturgy, Guidelines *Au cours des derniers mois*, to assist catechesis on the anaphoras of the Mass, 2 June 1968, in *Documents on the Liturgy 1963–1979: Conciliar, Papal and Curial Texts* [Collegeville, MN: Liturgical Press, 1982], 618 [DOL 244]).

of salvation history comes *in the context of a glorious proclamation of joy in God*, which imbues the entire prayer.

The preface, with its account of God, is not simply a page torn from a theology text. It is truly a "celebration of God"[8]—first, in God's own nature and then in God's works. Note, for example, the exuberance with which the prayer acclaims the holiness and goodness of creation, reminiscent of the beautiful Anaphora of St. James. That medieval prayer of the church in Jerusalem is stunning (in this passage from the beginning of the preface) in its lyrical praise of God in his creative work:

> It is truly right and fitting, suitable and profitable, to praise you, to hymn you, to bless you, to worship you, to glorify you, to give thanks to you, the creator of all creation, visible and invisible, the treasure of eternal good things, the fountain of life and immortality, the God and Master of all. You are hymned by the heaven of heavens and all their powers; the sun and moon and all the choirs of stars; earth, sea, and all that is in them. . . .[9]

The tone of both this prayer and Eucharistic Prayer IV, in which we "confess [God's] name in exultation," seems almost to demand exclamation points. But in speaking of the exuberance of Eucharistic Prayer IV, I refer to more than its tone. I speak also of its content, which is rich in references to joy, praise, and, most of all, glory.

The prayer is marked by joy. In the preface we proclaim that the *reason* for God's creative work was "so that you might fill your creatures with blessings and bring joy to many of them by the glory of your light." Though all the Roman anaphoras refer to Christ's dying and rising in the carrying out of his mission, only Eucharistic Prayer IV also speaks of his preaching, which is presented as joyous by its very nature: "To the poor, he proclaimed the good news of salvation, to prisoners, freedom, and to the sorrowful of heart, joy."

8. Mazza, *The Eucharistic Prayers*, 161.
9. Jasper and Cuming, *Prayers of the Eucharist*, 90.

The prayer is also marked by praise, which has a particularly strong role in the long section following the Sanctus, in a sense dominating it. The section opens by saying "We give you praise, Father most holy," and then it is as though the entire section that follows (33 lines in the English translation) presents the Trinity's saving work in history as the *reason* for our praise.[10]

Eucharistic Prayer IV is marked even more by the theme of glory. This is felt from its opening lines. It begins with the classic opening of the Roman prefaces, "It is truly right to give you thanks," but then immediately continues with an expression not found in them, that it is also "truly just to give you glory, Father most holy."

I pointed above to the preface's striking comment that God sent his Son in order to "bring joy"—note that the same line specifies that he brings this joy "by the glory of your light." Leading up to the Sanctus, where a reference to God's glory would be expected, the words of glory seem almost to trip over each other, speaking of the angels who "gazing upon the glory of your face, glorify you without ceasing."

Notice the introduction to the institution narrative, too. Each of the other Roman anaphoras here makes reference to Jesus' suffering.[11] Then there's Eucharistic Prayer IV: "When the hour had come for him to be glorified by you, Father most holy. . . ." Another place where glory's presence stands out is the second epiclesis, where we pray that God may gather into one body all who receive the Body and Blood of the Lord, "that . . . they may truly become a living sacrifice in Christ to the praise of your glory." The theme of glory is reinforced several other times in Eucharistic Prayer IV as well.

Pointing out these themes is not simply cherry-picking ideas that could be found in any anaphora. Some quick comparisons make clear how distinctive their presence is in Eucharistic Prayer IV. The word *joy* appears twice in Eucharistic Prayer IV; it is

10. Mazza, *The Eucharistic Prayers*, 164.
11. Eucharistic Prayer I: "On the day before he was to suffer . . ."; Eucharistic Prayer II: "At the time he was betrayed and entered willingly into his Passion . . ."; Eucharistic Prayer III: "For on the night he was betrayed. . . ."

completely absent from Prayers I, II, and III. *Praise* appears twice in Eucharistic Prayer IV (and the synonym *exultation* once); it is in each of the other three one time. While *glory* (or a form if it, such as *glorify*) appears in Eucharistic Prayer I and III three times each, and in Eucharistic Prayer II four times, it is in Eucharistic Prayer IV ten times!

Also related to Eucharistic Prayer IV's joyful exuberance is the strong presence of love. In all, *love* (or some form of it, such as *beloved*, *loving*, or translated as *charity*) appears in the anaphora five times. Compare this to its appearance not at all in Eucharistic Prayer I, twice in Eucharistic Prayer II, and once in Eucharistic Prayer III.

Praying for All God's People

There is still another distinctive feature of Eucharistic Prayer IV that we haven't mentioned yet. As with the salvation history element, it's helpful to see this too in the context of the prayer as a joyful praise of God's glory.

The intercessions of this anaphora are more wide-reaching than we typically find in the Roman rite. In the Roman Canon, with its strong ecclesial theme, the intercessions are a prayer for the church, its leaders, its people, in union with its saints. This is imitated in Eucharistic Prayers II and III, as well as in the other eucharistic prayers of the Roman rite.

But in Eucharistic Prayer IV we find an "openness not only to believers in Christ, but also to all people."[12] Its intercessions pray for the pope, bishop, and clergy, for those who make the offering and those who are gathered for it, for "your entire people" (the universal church)—and then comes the unique element: "and all who seek you with a sincere heart." Note, too, that according to the structure and punctuation of the intercessions (especially the colon in the second line, which is also in the Latin of the typical edition), we speak our conviction that those outside the institutional church who seek God with a sincere heart are

12. Marsili et al., *Eucaristia*, 254 (my translation).

included, with all the others named, among those "for whom we make this offering."

Mazza notes that the expression "has no parallel in the early anaphoric tradition."[13] But it is completely faithful to the ecclesiology of the Second Vatican Council, as expressed in the Dogmatic Constitution on the Church, *Lumen Gentium*:

> The Church knows that she is joined in many ways to the baptized who are honored by the name of Christian, but who do not however profess the Catholic faith in its entirety or have not preserved unity or communion under the successor of Peter. . . .
>
> Finally, those who have not yet received the Gospel are related to the People of God in various ways. [These include Jews and Muslims.] Nor is God remote from those who in shadows and images seek the unknown God. . . . Those who, through no fault of their own, do not know the Gospel of Christ or his Church, but who nevertheless seek God with a sincere heart, and, moved by grace, try in their actions to do his will as they know it through the dictates of their conscience—those too may achieve eternal salvation. (LG 15, 16)

This unique element of the intercessions in Eucharistic Prayer IV, then, might be seen as an apt liturgical expression of the dogmatic teaching of the church; if it is in some ways unprecedented, that could be because the manner of expression of the doctrine in the conciliar constitution is also in some ways new, or at least a retrieval of a theological approach that had been forgotten for many centuries.[14] The conviction is also reflected in Eucharistic Prayer IV's post-Sanctus, in the stanza related to the work of the Father, where we proclaim that God "came in mercy to the aid of all, so that those who seek might find you.")

---

13. Mazza, *The Eucharistic Prayers*, 188.

14. Cf. Yves M. J. Congar, "The People of God," in John H. Miller, ed., *Vatican II: An Interfaith Appraisal* (Notre Dame, IN: University of Notre Dame Press, 1966), 197–207.

The expression fits well within the context of the anaphora's joy in God. It is as though, in its exuberance, the prayer embraces all God's people more explicitly perhaps than any other anaphora in history.

Given all of this, the overall impression of Eucharistic Prayer IV is not simply of reciting a creed, but of rejoicing in the Good News it encapsulates. Eucharistic Prayer IV sees the creed as a wonderful expression of God's love and a revelation of God's glory, and the anaphora itself is the church's fitting response of praise.

The Nine Other Current Eucharistic Prayers of the Roman Rite

The four eucharistic prayers we've just considered have been the primary anaphoras of the Roman rite since 1969. Only these four are placed on the pages of the Roman Missal within the Order of Mass itself. But elsewhere in the Missal one can find several other eucharistic prayers that may be used on certain occasions. (How many others—six or nine—depends on whether one counts the Eucharistic Prayers for Various Needs and Occasions as one prayer or four. See below.) Though we could certainly spend much time considering the history and contents of each one, space considerations mean we'll have to be brief here.

Eucharistic Prayers for Masses of Reconciliation

A Year of Reconciliation

In a tradition that goes back at least seven hundred years, the Vatican marks every twenty-fifth year ('00, '25, '50, and '75) as a Holy Year, a special invitation to Catholics to draw closer to Christ through prayer, penance, and pilgrimage. The Jubilee Year 2000 was marked with extraordinary solemnity and celebration under the leadership of Pope John Paul II. The same pope had also proclaimed 1983 as a special Holy Year of Redemption, marking the 1,950th anniversary of the death and resurrection of Jesus. Before those was the Holy Year of 1975.

Pope Paul VI chose the theme of reconciliation as a special emphasis during that year. In order that it might "resound repeatedly"[1] (as the Vatican's Congregation for Divine Worship [CDW] put it) in the church's liturgy that year, and in response to requests from some bishops of the world, the pope gave permission for the composition of two new eucharistic prayers that reflected the theme of reconciliation.

The Eucharistic Prayers for Masses of Reconciliation (EPMR) were approved, together with three new Eucharistic Prayers for Masses with Children (EPMC), on 1 November 1974 on an experimental basis for a period of three years. The CDW permitted each bishops' conference to choose one from each of these sets of new prayers for use throughout its region, and it insisted that the EPMR could be used only "when there are special celebrations with the theme of reconciliation and penance, especially during Lent and on the occasion of a pilgrimage or religious meeting."[2]

At the end of 1977, after the initial three-year period, the CDW noted that the bishops' conferences where the prayers had been used had "nearly unanimously rendered a favorable judgment on their use,"[3] and permission was granted "experimentally" for another three years. Then in 1981 definitive permission was given for the use of all five special prayers throughout the world, and it was only at this point that they began to be included in each subsequent edition of the Sacramentary in English. In 1983 Pope John Paul II encouraged the use of the EPMR during the special Holy Year of Redemption.

With God and One Another, In Christ

Enrico Mazza writes that in the two EPMR the "aspect of reconciliation with the brethren [as opposed to reconciliation with God] received most attention."[4] I'd have to disagree with him here and suggest that it seems more the case that the first of

---

1. *Documents on the Liturgy 1963–1979: Conciliar, Papal, and Curial Texts* (Collegeville, MN: Liturgical Press, 1982), 634 (= DOL 250, no. 2024).

2. Ibid., 629 (= DOL 249, no. 1995).

3. Ibid., 634 (= DOL 251, no. 2028).

4. Enrico Mazza, *The Eucharistic Prayers of the Roman Rite*, tr. Matthew J. O'Connell (New York: Pueblo, 1986), 191.

the two prayers emphasizes reconciliation *with God* in Christ, while the second emphasizes reconciliation with *our neighbors* in Christ.

In Prayer I the scriptural idea of covenant takes a central place. The idea of the covenant between God and humanity, either that of the Old Testament or the new covenant ratified in the blood of Christ, runs like a golden strand throughout the anaphora. After humanity's failure to live up to its covenant with God, the prayer says, "through your Son, Jesus our Lord, you bound yourself even more closely with the human family by a bond that can never be broken." The Eucharist is referred to in this prayer as "the sacrifice which restores man to your friendship."

The covenant is not mentioned at all in Prayer II (except in the words of institution, which are identical in every eucharistic prayer of the 1969 Missal). After opening with reference to the "conflict and division" that trouble the human family, the prayer refers to the Spirit, by whose action "enemies begin to speak to one another, those who were estranged join hands in friendship, and nations seek the way of peace together." Through Christ's death we "find our way to one another," and we look forward to the day when God will "gather people of every race, language, and way of life to share in the one eternal banquet with Jesus Christ the Lord."

Eucharistic Prayers for Masses with Children

Not a Liturgical Text

In 1963, *Sacrosanctum Concilium* called for "provision [to] be made, when revising the liturgical books, for legitimate variations and adaptations to different groups, regions and peoples."[5] In a significant preliminary response the CDW published a *Directory for Masses with Children* on 1 November 1973. The directory observed that even though Mass could now be celebrated in the vernacular of each people, "still the words and signs have not

5. SC 38. Translation from Austin Flannery, OP, ed., *Vatican Council II: The Conciliar and Post-Conciliar Documents*, 1988 rev. ed. (Boston: St. Paul Editions, 1987).

been sufficiently adapted to the capacity of children."[6] It encouraged presiders at Masses where most of the assembly was made up of children to choose presidential texts that seem most suitable for children and to adapt these texts to the needs of children while "preserving the purpose of the prayer and to some extent its substance as well."[7] It then noted: "For the present, the four Eucharistic prayers approved by the supreme authority for Masses with adults and introduced into liturgical use are to be employed until the Apostolic See makes other provision for Masses with children."[8]

At the time of the directory's publication, work within the Consilium was already under way on the composition of eucharistic prayers intended for use in Masses with children, and precisely a year later, as noted above, three Eucharistic Prayers for Masses with Children were approved along with the two EPMR. The CDW explained the introduction of *three* anaphoras for children's Masses by saying that "it is very difficult for only one eucharistic prayer to be used throughout the world in Masses with children, in view of cultural differences and the mentality of various peoples."[9] (The directive that each bishops' conference choose one of the three for use in its territory seems to imply the somewhat naïve presumption that there are no such differences in culture or mentality within the bounds of a given conference's territory.)

The congregation emphasized that use of these anaphoras should be restricted to Masses where the majority of the assembly was made of up children. The EPMC represent an extraordinary moment in liturgical history: never before had an anaphora been designed specifically with the unique needs of one particular group within the church in mind.[10]

---

6. *Documents on the Liturgy*, 677 (= DOL 276, no. 2135).
7. Ibid., 687 (=DOL 276, no. 2184).
8. Ibid.
9. Ibid., 631 (= DOL 250, no. 2006).
10. Clare V. Johnson suggests that the presider's freedom to pray the anaphora extemporaneously during the first four centuries of the church might be considered a precedent in this regard, since we might say that the anaphora was then being adapted to the needs of the local community. It's not clear, of course, that presiders were particularly conscious of considering their local community's

Even more significantly, the CDW gave very wide latitude to translators of the EPMC into the local vernaculars: "In this case the Latin text is not intended for liturgical use. Therefore it is not to be merely translated." Latin style and structure were to be left aside, and the vernacular translations were to be "adapted to the spirit of the respective language as well as to the manner of speaking with children in each language concerning matters of great importance."[11] In another way, then, the EPMC represent a notable moment in liturgical history. The official Latin text is *not, strictly speaking, a liturgical text at all*. It is not a "typical edition" from which all translations must be rendered, but rather a model on which a direct composition in the vernacular of a given region would be based.[12] In a fascinating article, Clare V. Johnson has argued that the EPMC represent "a successful and concrete example of what today would be termed liturgical inculturation."[13]

Talking to Children about Important Things

ICEL has offered a generally successful English rendering of the prayers.[14] I offer my observations both as a student of the liturgy and as the father of seven children. All three are appropriately simple in vocabulary and ideas, concrete in expression, and reverent in tone. They seem truly to succeed in the CDW's intentions, noted above, of presenting their ideas in "the manner of speaking with children . . . concerning matters of great importance."[15]

Prayer I is both simple and beautiful. An interesting feature is its division of the Sanctus into two separate sections within

---

particular needs at the time. (Cf. Clare V. Johnson, "The Children's Eucharistic Prayers: A Model of Liturgical Inculturation," *Worship* 75, no. 3 [2001]: 209.)

11. *Documents on the Liturgy,* 631 (= DOL 250, no. 2009).

12. Cf. Johnson, "Children's Eucharistic Prayers," 211; Mazza, *The Eucharistic Prayers*, 238–39.

13. Johnson, "Children's Eucharistic Prayers," 211. See also Johnson's list of ten presumptions about children and their culture that apparently were made by the composers of these three prayers (pp. 217–23).

14. Since the Latin versions of these prayers are not intended as a liturgical text, but rather as a model for translation, the comments I offer here refer to the ICEL translations (as they exist at the date of this publication) in particular.

15. *Documents on the Liturgy*, 631 (=DOL 250, no. 2009).

the text of the preface. Somewhat oddly, the same preface includes intercessions for the church, the pope, and the local bishop (a feature typically found later, in the intercessions).

Prayer II is notable for the opportunity it offers for vocal participation by the assembly. It contains a total of ten additional acclamations.

Prayer III contains interesting variations, three of them, for use during the Easter season, but these seem almost to have been composed by a different redactor, and they are less successful because they are both less concrete and more complex.

With two exceptions, all three prayers include each of the important ideas of the various parts of the anaphora (preface, sanctus, etc.) in terms that children can understand. One exception is the omission of reference to the Holy Spirit in the first epiclesis of EPMC II, but this was corrected in the 2002 edition of the Roman Missal.

A second exception is the intercessions for the dead. These are absent from EPMC I and III. This omission seems unnecessary and even unfortunate. Children are aware when loved ones have died and do pray for them. Suggesting in the eucharistic prayer that there are dead we should pray for will not disturb them but rather will confirm, supplement, and put into action religious education received (one hopes) from parents and catechists.

The addition of many acclamations in these prayers (especially Prayer II) seems intended to foster greater vocal participation and probably to effectively address children's short attention spans. The CDW instruction even permits bishops' conferences to introduce other acclamations to the prayers, "provided they convey the same spirit."[16] We should acknowledge, however, that when the EPMC are used, these additional acclamations are often omitted, probably because explaining their inclusion to the children and preparing them to participate through these acclamations would demand significant time before the Mass itself. After all, since the prayers are only used in the uncommon instance of Masses in which children make up most of the assembly, even children from the most active Catholic families are bound to be unfamiliar with these

16. Ibid., 632 (= DOL 250, no. 2015).

anaphoras. The interjection of acclamations where they are not accustomed to hearing them at the Sunday Masses they usually attend will only come as a surprise, and perhaps even confuse them a bit. We might consider this aspect of these prayers a theoretically good idea, but unsuccessful in practice.

Eucharistic Prayers for Masses for Various Needs and Occasions

The "Swiss Anaphora"

The third edition of the Roman Missal includes the addition of another eucharistic prayer or—perhaps better—four more eucharistic prayers, which also have a unique history. In 1972 the dioceses of Switzerland observed an extraordinary national synod. The Swiss bishops requested Vatican approval for an anaphora composed on the occasion of that synod, which was granted on 8 August 1973.

Switzerland's unique linguistic culture no doubt contributed to what became the remarkable spread of this prayer to other countries. The nation is multilingual, and so the prayer appeared and was approved for use in that country in three different languages: German, French, and Italian. No typical Latin text existed.

Vatican permission for its use in one or another of its languages was soon sought and granted for Luxembourg in 1974; Austria and the Diocese of Strasburg in 1975; France, Belgium, Algeria, Morocco, and Tunisia in 1978; and more in subsequent years. Translations into *other* national languages were soon made, and permission for their use was also granted. For example, the use of a Hungarian translation was permitted in 1979; a Polish translation in 1984; and Spanish, Catalan, and Gallician translations for use in Spain in 1985. By 1989 the Vatican had approved the translation of the "Swiss" anaphora into twelve languages, for use in twenty-seven nations. As for an English translation, permission for its use was sought by and granted only to the bishops' conference of the Philippines.[17]

---

17. Corrado Maggioni, "Coordinate Spazio-Temporali della Preghiera Eucaristica 'Synode '72,'" *Notitiae* 27 (1991): 465–71.

It was only in 1991 that the Congregation for Divine Worship and the Discipline of the Sacraments published an official Latin text and gave it an official name, the Eucharistic Prayer for Various Needs and Occasions (EPVNO).[18] Among other things, this typical text harmonized the prayer a bit more with the other prayers of the Roman rite (incorporating, for example, the same introductory preface the others share and a similar transition from the Sanctus into the first epiclesis). With its addition to the Roman Missal of 2002 it was officially approved for use through-out the universal church.

Here we have a trajectory of development that is unique for the past thousand years and never followed in quite this way by any eucharistic prayer. An anaphora that was not given to the universal church by Rome, but rather composed for and by a particular church, was passed from particular church to particular church in the space of just a few years, with the approval of Rome, until it ultimately took its place in the universal patrimony of the Roman rite.[19]

Prayer for a Pilgrim Church

The unique structure makes it difficult to know whether to speak of one prayer or four; to me it seems more realistic to choose the latter. The prayers alternate between variable sections that are all their own and that express particular theological themes, and other sections that are common to all four of them. After the same introductory dialogue that is common to all of the other current Roman anaphoras there are four separate prefaces. Then, following the common Sanctus, comes a large section

18. The decree is also in *Notitiae* 27 (1991): 388–89. In the same issue Maggioni observed that the late appearance of the typical Latin text suggested that the widespread rush for permission to use the Swiss anaphora in so many other nations came as a surprise to the Vatican at the time (ibid., 469 n. 30). Previous to the official name given to the prayer at this time it had been known by several names in various countries and missals, such as "Eucharistic Prayer I" in the Italian missal, the Eucharistic Prayer "for Meetings" in the French missal, and even "Eucharistic Prayer VII" in the Hungarian missal (ibid., 471–72).

19. Ibid., 472–73.

that all share in common, which includes the first epiclesis (consecratory), the institution narrative, the memorial acclamation, the memorial-offering, and the second epiclesis (for unity). With the intercessions there are again four distinct parts, though the intercessions conclude with a block common to all four again, and then, continuing with the common block, the anaphoras close with the same doxology and amen.

Each prayer has its own title, expressing its theme:

> EPVNO I: The Church on the Way to Unity
> EPVNO II: God Guides the Church on the Way of Salvation
> EPVNO III: Jesus, the Way to the Father
> EPVNO IV: Jesus, the Compassion of God

Regarding the Sections Common to All Four

The imagery of human life and Christian faith as a *journey* is strong. Composed only a few years after the close of the Second Vatican Council, these prayers express a major theme of that council's teaching on the church; the seventh chapter of the Dogmatic Constitution on the Church (*Lumen Gentium*) is devoted to the idea of the pilgrim church. God is recognized as present to us in the midst of this journey, both in the past and in the present. Even Jesus' own paschal mystery is presented in the memorial section as a journey he made, led by the Father, through suffering to death and then resurrection, and finally to his Father's right hand.

EPVNO I: The Church on the Way to Unity

The ecclesiological theme is intense in this prayer. In fact, it is probably the only anaphora in history (and certainly the only one today) that makes no mention of angels in the introduction to the Sanctus; instead, it suggests that we join the praise of "all the Church" (with the implied presumption that the angels are a part of that church, perhaps) in proclaiming God's glory. In another expression of its unique ecclesiological preoccupation, it is also the only anaphora (again, perhaps in history) to provide a place (in the intercessions) for the specific mention of the diocese or place in which the Mass is being celebrated.

EPVNO II: God Guides the Church on the Way of Salvation

As the title suggests, the theme here is God's' divine providence in the history of his people. We see this strongly in the preface, which begins with the idea of God's providence in general (he is "creator of the world and source of all life"), moves on to cite his providence in the history of Israel, and finally proclaims that "you guide your pilgrim Church today as it journeys along the paths of time."

EPVNO III: Jesus, the Way to the Father

The fundamental theme in this prayer is Christ as the mediator. In the other three, for example, the preface opens by giving praise to the Father; in this one we praise the Father *through* Christ the Lord. Jesus is the Word made flesh, the "mediator who has spoken your words," and "the way that leads to you." This prayer is also notable for its references to the text of the Second Vatican Council's Pastoral Constitution on the Church in the Modern World (*Gaudium et Spes*).

EPVNO IV: Jesus, the Compassion of God

This prayer's expression of the compassion of God as expressed in the life and ministry of Jesus is beautifully scriptural. It subtly includes several key scriptural references to the compassion of Christ. For example, the preface includes a reference to the parable of the Good Samaritan, putting Jesus himself in the role of the Samaritan who stops along the way to help the hurting. Careful listeners will also hear in the intercessions indirect references to Matthew 11:28 ("Come to me, all you who labor and are burdened, and I will give you rest") and Christ's washing of the disciples' feet in John 13.[20]

---

20. Pere Tena, "Commentarium," *Notitiae* 27 (1991): 429.

Liturgy and Life

A Eucharistic Prayer Spirituality: Making the Church's Prayer Our Own

Pope St. Gregory the Great, in the late sixth century, spoke of the anaphora as simply the *prex*, or "prayer." The implication is that it is *the* prayer of the church, manifesting our relationship with God, our Christian identity, and our Christian life in a way that no other prayer does. It is the church's prayer *par excellence*. "[A]s such, this *prex* needs no qualifying adjective."[1]

If the eucharistic prayer is the church's prayer, it seems important that it serve as the *model of prayer* of each member of the church. If there is some element of my spiritual life that is not found in the eucharistic prayers of the church, surely it should be, at best, a peripheral element in my own prayer. If it contradicts the content and spirit of those prayers, I should probably rethink that aspect of my prayer life. On the other hand, what I find in those prayers I can safely incorporate into my own spirituality, as a child accepts food trustingly from its mother.

We occasionally hear calls for the renewal of a eucharistic spirituality among Catholics.[2] Paraphrasing Louis Bouyer (who was

1. Robert Cabie, *The Church at Prayer*, vol. 2: *The Eucharist*, new ed., tr. Matthew J. O'Connell (Collegeville, MN: Liturgical Press, 1986), 91. Cf. Robert McCarron, *The Eucharistic Prayer at Sunday Mass* (Chicago: Liturgy Training Publications, 1997), 50, 62.

2. E.g., Mark Brumley, "The Eucharist: Source and Summit of Christian Spirituality," at http://www.ignatiusinsight.com/features2005/brumley_eucharist1_aug05.asp, reprinting an article that originally appeared in *The Catholic Faith* (May/June 1996); Dominick D. Hankle, "Spirituality of the Eucharist," *Spiritual Life* (Winter 2001): 222–31.

talking about theology rather than spirituality), there is a "great gulf" between the many eucharistic spiritualities and what alone deserves to be called the spirituality of the Eucharist, meaning a spirituality that is rooted in the church's eucharistic prayer.[3]

When Pope John Paul II, in an apostolic letter marking the fortieth anniversary of *Sacrosanctum Concilium*, called for a renewed "liturgical spirituality," he insisted that it would come about only through a rediscovery of "*the art of 'mystagogic catechesis,'* so dear to the Fathers of the Church."[4] He was referring to the ancient style of teaching and preaching left to us by Cyril of Jerusalem, Ambrose, John Chrysostom, Theodore of Mopsuestia, and others.[5] In some extraordinary sets of catechetical homilies, these great shepherds explained the mysteries of the Christian faith to the newly baptized through *reflection on the liturgical rites themselves*.

What would an authentic Catholic spirituality rooted in the eucharistic prayer look like? There are surely as many different prayer lives as there are people who pray. But I'd like to suggest ten characteristics that will be incorporated in some way into the spirituality of a Christian who allows himself or herself to be *formed by liturgical engagement with the current eucharistic prayers of the Roman rite*. I've already touched on many of these elsewhere in this book; others, though, have received less attention.

1. A Eucharistic Prayer Spirituality Is Eucharistic, in the Original Sense of the Term

Giving thanks is what gives the prayer (which was called *Eucharist* before the sacrament, the rite of the sacrament, or the consecrated elements were) its name. Can there be any doubt

3. Cf. Louis Bouyer, *Eucharist: Theology and Spirituality of the Eucharistic Prayer*, tr. Charles Underhill Quinn (Notre Dame, IN: University of Notre Dame Press, 1968), 5.

4. Pope John Paul II, *Spiritus et Sponsa*, 12, 16 (emphasis in the original).

5. Cf. Edward Yarnold, SJ, *The Awe-Inspiring Rites of Initiation: The Origins of the R.C.I.A.*, 2d ed. (Collegeville, MN: Liturgical Press, 1994); Enrico Mazza, *Mystagogy: A Theology of Liturgy in the Patristic Age*, tr. Matthew J. O'Connell (New York: Pueblo, 1989).

that the eucharistic prayer is about expressing our gratitude to God for the good he has done for us in Christ?

If giving joyful thanks to God "always and everywhere" grounds the praying of the prayer and the celebration of Mass, it is also the foundation of a Christian spirituality based on the eucharistic prayer. This is strikingly consistent with the spirituality that emerges from the New Testament, and in particular the writings of St. Paul.

Living life can be difficult business, and it's an understatement to say that for some people it is understandably experienced at times as less than a gift. The eucharistic prayer challenges us to see the most dour elements of our lives relative to and in the light of God's great gifts to us. It may help to remember that it is not for daily pleasures and joys that we give thanks in the eucharistic prayer, but for the *mirabila dei*, God's great wonderworks—creation and redemption.

2. A Eucharistic Prayer Spirituality Is Christic

I was going to call this characteristic "christocentric," but the term seems not quite to describe the nature of the eucharistic prayer. Prayed (in the words of the doxology) "through [Christ], with [Christ], and in [Christ]," offering "all glory and honor" to the Father, the eucharistic prayer offers Christians an opportunity to become co-pray-ers with Christ.

I have no interest in criticizing worship of Christ the Lord or prayer addressed *to* Christ (indeed, these are part of my own prayer life). But it seems that a spirituality formed by the eucharistic prayer will be marked by a strong awareness of living the whole of one's life, including one's spiritual life, *in* Christ. It will mean being able to say, ever more truly, with Paul, "Christ lives in me and I in him."

More specifically, the eucharistic prayer, which is so intensely anamnetic, will always draw those who are formed by it more deeply into suffering, dying, and rising with Christ. It should help us to be more aware that when life is difficult and burdensome we suffer in him and he in us; to see our inevitable death as a sharing in his own; and to see, permeating it all, a sublime hope of sharing in his resurrection.

3. A Eucharistic Prayer Spirituality Is Filial

Nothing is clearer in the gospels than the fact that Christ's whole life was lived in relation to his heavenly Father, and that his prayer was an expression of his intense union with the Father. These same qualities mark the anaphoras themselves just as clearly. Any authentic Christian spirituality, and certainly one that is formed by the eucharistic prayers, will have the Father of Jesus as its focus and end. This means relating to God primarily as a daughter or son, and allowing one's awareness of sonship/daughtership to permeate one's whole life.

A corollary of this is that we will also see God's people as brothers and sisters and relate to them as God's "children" and fellow members of the "family" God has called together.[6] This can sound almost quaint, but so much of our culture, politics, and history trains us to see one another as opponents, competitors, rivals, and takers.

4. A Eucharistic Prayer Spirituality Is Pneumatological

The robust epicleses of some anaphoras of the liturgical tradition leave no doubt that the Holy Spirit is the fuel and the engine to the transubstantiation of the bread and wine, as well as the sanctification and unification of the church, that come as a result of the eucharistic prayer. For that matter, the Spirit is also the source of our giving thanks, our praise, our keeping memorial, and our intercessions. For the eucharistic prayer, the Spirit is behind it all.

With the anaphora at the heart of our spiritual lives we become keenly aware that our relationship with God is not something we achieve by our own efforts, but rather something we receive as a gift of the Spirit. For "[us], who are . . . filled with

---

6. Eucharistic Prayer III, second epiclesis.

the Holy Spirit,"[7] time and effort put into prayer is not working toward improving our relationship with God. It is, rather, opening ourselves ever more generously to the Spirit's work in us.

5. A Eucharistic Prayer Spirituality Is Ecclesial

Even a priest who offers Mass by himself in a tiny chapel is praying in union with the whole church—the church in heaven as well as the church scattered around the earth; the church today as well as the church that has offered the Mass throughout the past two millennia, all made one in Christ! The eucharistic prayer is never *my* prayer, always *our* prayer.

So our entire Christian lives, including our spirituality, should be inherently ecclesial. That's not to say we should never pray by ourselves, but rather that our personal prayer should push us always toward others, toward the community that is the church and the faith that is the church's, and especially toward the Sunday eucharistic assembly which manifests the church as nothing else does.[8] A spirituality formed by the eucharistic prayer will never allow an attitude that says "I'm just concerned about saving my own soul—to hell with the world."

Further, this ecclesiality is not earthbound. The saints will be vibrantly present in the spiritual life of one who is formed by the eucharistic prayer, and we will live the whole of our lives "in communion with those whose memory we venerate."[9]

6. A Eucharistic Prayer Spirituality Is Priestly

Echoing the Constitution on the Liturgy, the General Instruction of the Roman Missal insists that each of us "learn to offer [our]selves" at Mass.[10] The "spiritual significance"[11] of members of the assembly presenting the gifts to the priest for use at the altar extends outside the church building.

7. Eucharistic Prayer III, second epiclesis.
8. Cf. SC 41.
9. Eucharistic Prayer I, *Communicantes*.
10. GIRM 95.
11. GIRM 73.

This aspect of the Eucharist has been emphasized by the 1969 reform with the restoration of the ancient presentation of the gifts by the faithful just before the eucharistic prayer is prayed. For a group of laypeople to get up from their seats and carry forward to the priest the gifts to be offered is a beautiful expression of the idea that all of us offer ourselves to the Father with Christ in the Eucharist. Even though not all can participate in the actual procession, it should become a reminder to the rest of us who watch it happen, just as we are about to begin the eucharistic prayer, that during the prayer it should happen spiritually in each of our hearts.

7. A Eucharistic Prayer Spirituality Is Doxological

All thirteen of the current eucharistic prayers of the Roman rite open and close by glorifying God. So does almost every one of the eucharistic prayers of the church's long and diverse liturgical tradition. This is surely weighty data about what a spirituality based on the eucharistic prayer will include.

One need not be a "charismatic" in order to glorify God in one's prayer, any more than one need be a charismatic in order to pray the eucharistic prayers of Mass. If simply glorifying God seems somehow to be on the periphery of Catholic prayer, perhaps it is because Catholic prayer has too often been allowed to lose touch with the prayer of the church that is the anaphora. There is no reason that a Christian could not use the very text of the Sanctus or the doxology in one's own personal prayer.

8. A Eucharistic Prayer Spirituality Meets God in Creation

The prefaces of the eucharistic prayers in use today, like many from the liturgical tradition, give thanks to God, "creator of the world and source of all life,"[12] not only for the work of redemption, but also for the wonderful work of creation. Surely, then, a

---

12. Eucharistic Prayer for Various Needs and Occasions: God Guides the Church on the Way of Salvation, preface.

grateful appreciation of creation, and of the "wisdom and love"[13] with which God fashioned it, will be part of any spirituality that is shaped by the eucharistic prayer.[14]

We must remember that the eucharistic prayer is simply a text we speak aloud. The context in which it is spoken can be important. One obvious part of that context is that it is a prayer spoken over gifts of bread and wine. We rely in our liturgy on the gifts of creation (wheat and grapes, enhanced by human work), which ordinarily offer nourishment to our bodies, and we offer these gifts to God, who transforms them into nourishment for our spiritual lives and signs of the life of the new creation we're called to share in eternally.

9. A Eucharistic Prayer Spirituality Is Eschatological

I'm not the first to point out that a hymn whose lyrics proclaim proudly that our hope is "not in some heaven light years away" should make Christians uncomfortable. For a Catholic whose spirituality is formed by the eucharistic prayer, it's baffling. Primarily through the Sanctus, but also in other aspects, the anaphora reminds us that this world is not our homeland. Our participation in the liturgy is a foretaste and promise of the life we're called to live eternally in God. If Theodore of Mopsuestia's description of the Eucharist as "this solemn liturgy which leads us to such great hopes"[15] is accurate, our participation in it and reflection on it will increase our expectation of and longing for heaven.

10. A Eucharistic Prayer Spirituality Is Engaged with the World

Having our minds on the next world does not mean for a moment that we're unconcerned about the one we're living in. The vision of the kingdom of God that the liturgy affords us

13. Eucharistic Prayer IV, preface.

14. Cf. Denis Edwards, "Eucharist and Ecology: Keeping Memorial of Creation," *Worship* 82 (May 2008): 194–213.

15. Yarnold, *Awe-Inspiring Rites of Initiation*, 228.

provides even deeper motivation to attend to social needs and issues. Kevin Irwin writes: "Because even this graced world is imperfect and because the kingdom manifest in the liturgy is not yet fully realized in all of life, the liturgy implies and requires that those who participate in liturgy seek to extend the kingdom's manifestation here and now."[16] We see this expressed in the Eucharistic Prayer for Various Needs and Occasions IV, the intercessions of which ask God: "Keep your church alert in faith to the signs of the times and eager to accept the challenge of the gospel. Open our hearts to the needs of all humanity, so that sharing their grief and anguish, their joy and hope, we may faithfully bring them the good news of salvation and advance together on the way to your kingdom."

❑ ❑ ❑

One thing that strikes me as I review these categories is that they seem like a particularly Pauline list. The themes I've highlighted here as being prominent in the current eucharistic prayers are also prominent in the writings of St. Paul. It's not difficult, based on those very writings, to believe that Paul's faith and spirituality were formed in a fundamental way by his experience of the church's Eucharist.

---

16. Kevin W. Irwin, *Context and Text: Method in Liturgical Theology* (Collegeville, MN: Liturgical Press, 1994), 332.

Living an "Anaphoral" Life

The oldest surviving account of the death of a Christian martyr is known as *The Martyrdom of Polycarp*. It was written very soon after the event actually happened, around 156, and some of the details (like Polycarp grazing his shin as he steps from the carriage that transported him after his arrest) suggest it's at least partly based on an eyewitness account. Reading it prayerfully can be a wonderful experience for any Christian.

But one beautiful aspect of it is not immediately clear to the casual reader, and only research into liturgical history unveils it to us: the prayer the narrative puts on the lips of Polycarp at the moment of his death for Christ is based directly on the anaphora he would have uttered each time he led the church of Smyrna in its offering of the Eucharist.

An Anaphora in Fire

Polycarp was born around 70 AD. As a young man he became a student of the apostle John. Later, Polycarp would himself become the teacher of Irenaeus of Lyons, whose writings remain today a theological and historical treasure. By the beginning of the second century Polycarp was the bishop of the church in Smyrna (today the city of Izmir in Turkey); it was around this time that John wrote the Apocalypse, or Book of Revelation, which includes an important message addressed to "the angel of the church in Smyrna" (Rev 2:8-11).

In 107 Polycarp's remarkable story intersected with that of another great witness of the early church, Ignatius of Antioch.

Ignatius had also been a student of John, though earlier than Polycarp. He went on to lead the Christian community in Antioch not long after St. Peter himself left that city for Rome. Now a revered bishop, Ignatius had been arrested and sent in chains to Rome, where he would be executed. Crowds gathered along the roadsides to watch the entourage pass. They prayed, encouraged him, and some approached to kiss his chains. Ignatius wrote several letters during this journey that still exist and provide valuable insights into the life and faith of the church at the time. Along the way the guards stopped with their prisoner for several weeks in Smyrna, where Ignatius was permitted to stay in the home of Polycarp. Bishops and ordinary Christians from all around came to Polycarp's home to visit Ignatius. Once back on the road, Ignatius sent a letter back to Polycarp, which also still exists.[1]

Several decades later, in 156, Polycarp, now 86 years old, also faced death for his faith. *The Martyrdom of Polycarp* reports that the elderly bishop tried to avoid capture but was eventually arrested. His presence before the people assembled to witness the executions that day whipped the crowds into a frenzy. Exhorted to "curse the Christ," Polycarp asked, "How can I blaspheme my king who saved me?" He was threatened first with wild beasts and then, when that did not move him, with fire. "Bring what you will," he said as the crowds cried for his blood.

The martyrdom account says that as the logs began to burn, a fragrance like incense spread around Polycarp (note the liturgical reference), and he began to pray. The prayer that is recorded as coming from his mouth at this moment—as Polycarp was, it

---

1. On Ignatius of Antioch see Mike Aquilina, *The Fathers of the Church*, expanded ed. (Huntington, IN: Our Sunday Visitor, 2006), 59–66. The letters of Ignatius can be found at http://www.earlychristianwritings.com/ignatius (accessed 8/12/09). On Polycarp see Aquilina, *Fathers*, 67–72. *The Martyrdom of Polycarp* can be found at http://www.earlychristianwritings.com/martyrdom-polycarp (accessed 8/12/09). The portion of the document that includes Polycarp's prayer is in Enrico Mazza, *The Celebration of the Eucharist: The Origin of the Rite and the Development of Its Interpretation*, tr. Matthew J. O'Connell (Collegeville, MN: Liturgical Press, 1999), 312–14. See also Rod Bennett, *Four Witnesses: The Early Church in Her Own Words* (San Francisco: Ignatius Press, 2002), 95–152.

says, "like a loaf baking in the oven"—is the adaptation of what
was surely a eucharistic prayer of the Christian liturgy of that
time. In fact, it is (Enrico Mazza points out)[2] remarkably close
in structure and theme to the anaphora we find in the *Apostolic
Tradition*.

In his prayer, Polycarp, raising his eyes to heaven, blesses the
Father and gives thanks for the knowledge of him that comes
through his Son Jesus. He closes with a beautiful doxology that
leads up to an Amen. But in between there is "one important
change"[3] from what we find in the *Apostolic Tradition*: where the
latter prayer provides the narrative of Christ instituting the Lord's
Supper, we find Polycarp giving thanks for his martyrdom.

Object if you want that it may not have actually happened this
way, the holy bishop praying aloud an extended prayer as the
flames rose around him. If it didn't, the insight comes from the
author of the account rather than Polycarp himself, but it's just as
worthwhile: there is a "special connection between the Eucharist
and martyrdom."[4] Speaking more generally, the Mass we celebrate
and in particular the anaphora we pray there *has consequences in
and is manifested by the lives we live as Christians.* It calls us to "a
profound harmony between worship and life, between spirituality
and liturgy, between Eucharistic rite and ethical commitment."[5]

In chapter 1 we considered the ancient adage *lex orandi, lex
credendi*: The law of prayer establishes the law of belief. Our liturgical prayer is the foundation of the content of our Christian faith.
The account of Polycarp's martyrdom teaches us in a dramatic
way that the *lex orandi* and the *lex credendi* lead us necessarily to
a *lex vivendi*—a "law of living."[6] In other words, our liturgical
prayer establishes not only what we believe but also the way we
live (and as we suggested in chapter 1, what is true of the liturgy

2. Enrico Mazza, *The Origins of the Eucharistic Prayer*, tr. Ronald E. Lane
(Collegeville, MN: Liturgical Press, 1995), 154–56.

3. Mazza, *Celebration of the Eucharist*, 135.

4. Ibid.

5. Ibid., 137.

6. Cf. Kevin Irwin, *Context and Text: Method in Liturgical Theology* (Collegeville,
MN: Liturgical Press, 1994), 331.

in general is true in a particular way of the eucharistic prayer). If it doesn't, something important is missing.

Pope Benedict expresses the same insight when he writes of the "intrinsically eucharistic nature of Christian life." The Eucharist, he says, "embraces the concrete, everyday existence of the believer."[7] Let's consider for a moment how it does so, specifically as that applies to the anaphora we pray when we gather for Mass.

What We Bring to the Table

We spoke in chapter 2 of the priesthood of the baptized, by virtue of which all the faithful are called to "participate in the offering of the Eucharist."[8] In that chapter, and again in chapter 9, I cited a beautiful passage from *Lumen Gentium* that also bears repeating here to make another important point:

> For all their works, prayers and apostolic undertakings, family and married life, daily work, relaxation of mind and body, if they are accomplished in the Spirit—indeed even the hardships of life if patiently borne—all these become spiritual sacrifices acceptable to God through Jesus Christ (cf. [1] Pet 2:5). In the celebration of the Eucharist these may most fittingly be offered to the Father along with the body of the Lord. And so, worshipping everywhere by their holy actions, the laity consecrate the world itself to God.[9]

Earlier we considered it to help reinforce the idea that the laity are truly offerers of the eucharistic sacrifice. Here I want to point out that the council *presumes*, in presenting this idea, that we're living an apostolic life outside of the church building as we go about our daily lives. Our liturgical participation is considered *in the context of* our works, prayers, apostolic undertakings, family life, patience in hardship, and the rest. We bring these matters of

---

7. Pope Benedict XVI, Post-synodal Apostolic Exhortation *Sacramentum Caritatis*, 71.

8. LG 10.

9. LG 34.

daily life with us to offer at the eucharistic table, along with the eucharistic Christ.

If we're living lives full of selfishness, hatred, discriminations, injustices, infidelities, and sins for which we have no repentance, that's what we bring to the table. Is this what we want to offer to the Father? In fact, is it any wonder that, with this in mind, the Roman Canon is so preoccupied with the idea of our making an *acceptable* offering to the Lord? (See chapter 13.)

Praying the anaphora, in other words, is easy. But praying it authentically, so that in praying it we make an offering of ourselves, with Christ, to the Father, and so that the offering we make is a pure and acceptable sacrifice (like those of Abel, Abraham, and Melchizedek) and not a self-accusation that at best makes fools of us—that is a herculean task.

The Anaphora's Challenge of Justice

As we consider the lives we live outside of Mass, we can't ignore the fact that we live them in the context of "a society that lives by discriminations, by weaving the fabric of society around the difference between master and slave, man and woman, citizen and noncitizen, householder and migrant worker."[10] The eucharistic prayer offers significant insights about such circumstances and what it means to live as a Christian in the midst of them.

Early in the anaphora we sing the Sanctus, joining the angels of heaven in the praise of God's glory. This glimpse through heaven's front door strengthens our eschatological hope for the day when God's kingdom will come in its fullness and God will be all in all. But angelic songs of glory are only one aspect of the eschatological vision of the Bible. Jesus' vision of the end-times included the divine judgment of each person, followed by eternal reward or punishment. And the criterion on which this judgment will be based is whether we have fed the hungry, given drink to the thirsty, welcomed the stranger, clothed the naked, cared for

---

10. David N. Power, "The Eucharistic Table: In Communion with the Hungry," *Worship* 83 (September 2009): 388.

the ill, visited the imprisoned. Singing those glorious and eternal songs of praise, this other vision of the end-times insists, will be lost to those who have ignored these works of justice.

So our ideas about the eschatological nature of the Eucharist are incomplete if we only rejoice in joining the angels' song. The Eucharist must also become a profound call to make the ultimate overcoming of the world's miseries and injustices a reality, however incomplete, today. "The eschatological expectation of a new heaven and a new earth is proclaimed in the hope of a time when all are fed and when humanity and creation are one and at peace, of which each Eucharist is to be a sacrament and a pledge."[11] Saying that our celebration of the Eucharist puts us in the astonishing position of "standing with one foot on earth and one foot in heaven" is not just a joyful proclamation; it also sets a high bar and offers a daunting challenge. It's no wonder, then, that Kevin Irwin insists: "It is eschatology that grounds the ethical dimension of liturgy by linking liturgy with life here and now, particularly in linking liturgy with social justice, mission, service, and love."[12]

Besides the Sanctus, other aspects of every eucharistic prayer we pray serve as a call to a stronger commitment to works of justice and peace. We pray the epiclesis and the institution narrative and then recognize, adore, and receive the presence of Christ in the eucharistic elements. But do we have the right to pick and choose between the types of Christ's presence among us that we prefer to acknowledge? Can we rejoice and adore the presence of Christ in what was once bread and wine, but ignore his presence in the poor and the sick? To be sure, that presence is different in nature, but it is nonetheless real in both cases. Christ's own words about our encounter with him in the poor and sorrowful are strong and insistent, even quasi-sacramental. Hence the teaching of the *Catechism of the Catholic Church*: "The Eucharist commits us to the poor. To receive in truth the Body and Blood of Christ given up for us, we must recognize Christ in the poorest."[13]

---

11. Ibid., 391.
12. Irwin, *Context and Text*, 332.
13. CCC 1397.

Speaking of the institution narrative, Father Frank Pavone, national director of Priests for Life, has noted the supreme and sad irony that the phrase "this is my body" finds a central place in the Christian Eucharist, expressing Christ's ultimate selflessness and making him present among us, and also serves as a rallying cry in support of a right to legal abortion, framing such an act as an expression of a woman's freedom to do what she wishes with her own body.[14] And yet abortion is, at least objectively, a profoundly selfish act, one that ignores the fundamental rights and dignity of some of the least powerful among us—those who are, by that fact, truly Christ in our midst.

I refer just above to the first epiclesis, which calls upon the Spirit to transform the bread and wine into the body and blood of Christ. But there is also the second epiclesis, in which we ask the Spirit to make us one body in Christ. Surely to ask for such unity implies a prayer that all discriminations and unjust inequalities among us be overcome.[15] And how arrogant we are if we pray for this to happen, but then step back into our daily lives only to ignore the ways in which these injustices persist among us.

Then, too, there is the very bread and wine we place on our altar and over which we pray our anaphora, leading ultimately to their consumption. If we stop to think about it, shouldn't it make us a little uncomfortable that we have both the time and the resources to gather in a relaxed, clean, and quiet setting every Sunday around a table with food and drink we're able to produce/purchase readily and to set aside for no other purpose than our community worship? Certainly eating the Communion hosts and taking a little sip from a chalice offers little physical nourishment. Our food and drink here have a completely spiritual purpose. We use it not for physical nourishment, but for prayer.

Putting our food and drink to sacred use is no sin. But shouldn't it at least give us pause to consider that we're usually able to do it without longing for just a few more bites of that bread in order to

14. http://www.priestsforlife.org/brochures/thisismy.html (accessed 8/28/09).
15. Power, "The Eucharistic Table," 388.

satisfy our hunger pains, and without thinking that our distressing thirst could be alleviated if only we drank a few more gulps from the chalice? Shouldn't it induce just a bit of anxiety to remind ourselves that we pray over our bread, stored in most western sacristies in plastic bags stuffed with hosts, and our wine, stacked by the case in the sacristy closet—and even connect this sacred ritual with a claim to be a community of selfless love and service after the example of Christ, while millions are starving as we pray?

Praying the eucharistic prayer calls us to lives of justice and peace because the alternative is the scandal of praying the eucharistic prayer and *not* living such lives:

- It would mean praying Eucharistic Prayer I, calling our Eucharist a sacrifice of praise—which, we have seen, implies that our attitudes, hearts, and lives are consistent with our worship—and making a mockery of the statement. Are we prepared to compare, in that anaphora, our sacrifice to that of Abel, when it is really more like Cain's?
- It would mean praying Eucharistic Prayer II, proclaiming that Christ, by his paschal mystery, has "[broken] the bonds of death," while being content to live amidst the satanic bonds that imprison so many in our world—literal bondage like slavery, racism, and economic oppression, as well as spiritual bondage to and through our many other sins.
- It would mean praying Eucharistic Prayer III, asking the Father to "make of us an eternal offering," and then living as though our lives are anything but an offering to the Father; praying for "the peace and salvation of all the world," while ignoring the violence and sin of the world; and asking God to "confirm [the church] in faith and charity," while refusing to live lives of charity ourselves.
- It would mean praying Eucharistic Prayer IV, proclaiming that Christ came to announce "to the poor . . . the good news of salvation, to prisoners, freedom, and to the sorrowful of heart, joy," but arrogantly living as though such announcements ended with Christ and have little to do with our own Christian calling.

The eucharistic prayer we pray each Sunday offers all the elements we need of what Pope Benedict has called "a eucharistic spirituality capable of changing the fabric of society."[16]

❑ ❑ ❑

Eucharist, Mass, Divine Liturgy, Lord's Supper—there are many terms for this sacrament, whose central moment we have been exploring in this book. Here's one more term for it: *Life*.

That, in their own language, is the term fourth-century Punic people used to speak of it. St. Augustine, reporting this, added that he thought they were "perfectly correct" in their choice of terminology.[17]

We can agree, because praying the anaphora authentically means living an anaphoral life, one that does not make a sham of what we do and say around the altar.

16. Pope Benedict XVI, World Day of Peace Message 2009 ("Fighting Poverty to Build Peace"), available at http://www.vatican.va/holy_father/benedict_xvi/messages/peace/documents/hf_ben-xvi_mes_20081208_xlii-world-day-peace_en.html (accessed 9/9/09), cited in ibid., 394.

17. Mazza, *Celebration of the Eucharist*, 123 n. 21; 158 n. 66.